ILLUSTRATED
BASKETBALL COACHING
TECHNIQUES

ILLUSTRATED
BASKETBALL COACHING
TECHNIQUES

GARLAND F. PINHOLSTER
Basketball Coach
Oglethorpe (Ga.) University

Author of ENCYCLOPEDIA OF
BASKETBALL DRILLS

Illustrated by
Caroline Pinholster

PRENTICE-HALL, INC., *Englewood Cliffs, N.J.*

PRINTED IN THE UNITED STATES OF AMERICA

45090—BC

This book is dedicated to the 1958-59 Georgia Inter-Collegiate Athletic Conference basketball champions. These Oglethorpe University players also maintained the lowest defensive average of any team in the nation during the years 1951-60.

BILLY CARTER	FRANKIE LENTZ
ROGER COUCH	JOHN MOBLEY
WAYNE DOBBS	TOMMY NORWOOD
JAY DYE	JAY ROWLAND
SAMMY HUDGINS	PAT STEPHENS, JR.

Managers

BILL CHRISTIAN
BOB OLSON

Acknowledgment

The author of a sports book is indebted to all coaches and players who have preceded him and to those coaches and players who are active during his time. In writing this book we have tried to get the best ideas from each individual and from each era.

I am particularly grateful to Coach Adolph Rupp for endorsing this book. He has done more for the game of basketball than any other single person; his endorsement means much to me.

Steve Schmidt (Oglethorpe '41) has provided me with materials, inspiration and help throughout my tenure at Oglethorpe. He devised and produced a diagram stamp for this book that accelerated its production.

My wife has actually produced the "bread and butter" of the book. Without the illustrations, it would serve little purpose. We hope the text coupled with her tireless illustrating will serve as a tangible aid to all "basketball people" everywhere.

Preface

In order to be a successful coach today, you must not only have good material but you must have the best information that you can receive in order to develop this material.

Far too many coaches are complacent and take things as they are, while others are always eager to learn everything they can about the new techniques in basketball.

This new book, "Illustrated Basketball Coaching Techniques," by Coach Pinholster, vividly illustrates how to teach the basic fundamental skills. This should be a tremendous aid to everyone in our profession.

ADOLPH F. RUPP,
Basketball Coach
University of Kentucky
Lexington, Kentucky

Table of Contents

CONTENTS

Part I

THE LEARNING PROCESS

1. The Coach as Teacher

Successful coaches may employ widely different procedures. No one system holds the answer for every coach. There is no all-winning system. However, a great majority of successful coaches adhere to certain basic policies.

Probably the most important basic element in coaching is the coach's approach to teaching. *Successful coaches are good teachers.* There are those who may not think of themselves in that exact way. Yet, a close look at their procedures will prove, usually, that they do more and better teaching in many cases than the successful classroom instructor. The two words "coach" and "teacher" should be synonymous. In normal usage they often paint different pictures. All too often the coach considers coaching and teaching two different professions, but the two cannot be separated.

How many classroom teachers subscribe to four or five professional periodicals? Many coaches subscribe to more than that number of publications written with the definite aim of helping coaches improve themselves. They not only receive these materials but they study them avidly. How many teachers of academic subjects toss and turn sleeplessly all night trying to think of better procedures for getting their subjects across to their students? Many coaches are guilty of such devotion to the task.

Let us grant, then, than the good coach is actually a good teacher, even though he may not realize this. He will get better results if he recognizes this fact and exploits good teaching tech-

niques overtly and consciously. If the coach will come to think
of himself as a teacher, his methods will become more positive
and productive. He will communicate better with his players.
His players will have more respect for him.

The athletes have already developed many good habits in
the classroom that should not be wasted. The coach should capitalize on these habits by using methods similar to those of the
classroom. He should couple the best of the classroom teaching
tactics with the best of the traditional coaching techniques. His
class will then be held in an almost ideal learning climate; yet,
it will be informal enough to enjoy a period of laughter or a slang
expression at times. Slang expressions should not be continually
used, nor should "horseplay" be tolerated while class is in session.
A happy balance between academic formality and athletic in-
formality will result in the best possible learning environment.

The good academic teacher dos not allow people to wander in
and out of his classroom. He strongly discourages whispering or
talking while instruction is being given. He allows spectators to
visit who are courteous, tactful and *quiet*. He does not expect
students to gaze out of the window during instruction. He will
give the opportunity for laughter if something humorous occurs
occasionally. This entire atmosphere should be recreated during
the course of practice sessions. There will be more movement,
there will be somewhat more noise; however, the courtesy extended from teacher to student and from student to teacher
should be just as much in evidence.

The good classroom teacher has a lesson outlined or planned
that he follows. He is not bound completely by such an outline;
he uses it as insurance to make sure that the material to be
covered in the course and day by day is actually covered. This
technique of academic instruction is a "must" for the athletic
instructor. It is virtually impossible for the coach to cover all
phases of basketball during a season of play without some over-all
plan. Without one it is highly probable that he will be surprised
one evening, unprepared for a zone, press or freeze situation.
With an over-all plan, supplemented by daily and weekly sched-
ules, his team should never be surprised. They will have been
introduced to every tactical situation that could conceivably

create confusion or lack of confidence. They will have practiced every fundamental.

The good teacher is a good counselor. He always has an open ear and a warm response to the personal problems of his students. Coaches tend to take such counseling for granted as a part of their jobs. The truth is that few of us are capable of filling this role as it should be done. Sympathetic cluckings and a pat on the back are not enough. An efficient counselor spends many hours of study and many hours of thought upon understanding young-sters and their problems. If you sometimes weary of the parade of troubles laid at your feet by the team members, remember that you are actually being complimented. Students will not discuss private problems with someone they do not respect.

If each of the above methods is used, you will find many com-pensations other than improvement of the ball club. You will gain the respect of your contemporary teachers. They will understand you and your aims better. It will be much easier to talk to your players about the importance of their academic performances. You can sell them much easier on the value of becoming good students as well as good athletes. Incidentally, you will find that they usually become better athletes as a result of becoming better students.

It is not being suggested here that the coach become a stilted, formal, unhumorous clipboard character. It is simply suggested that we as coaches continue to use the best of our traditional methods along with the best classroom methods, to produce the most effective coaching techniques possible.

2. Learning Factors

The technical process of learning is very complicated. Many volumes have been written on the subject. All that will be attempted here is a brief sketch of the essentials involved in learning. The first section will be general and devoted to learning of all types. A more particular consideration is given to motor learning in the second section, which concerns the acquisition of skills. A summary is offered to give coaches the implications of learning that are particularly related to athletics.

Motivation

An important necessity for efficient learning, or perhaps for any type of learning, is motivation. Rewards of one kind or another cause men to put increased energies and efforts into their projects. Some rewards are more effective than others. The average man who has acquired a standard of living which satisfies his physical needs is motivated by both intrinsic and extrinsic rewards. The *intrinsic* represents such things as social recognition. The *extrinsic* represents material items which most men desire, such as money.

Types of Rewards

The use of *punishment* has been the focal point for widespread experimentation and conjecture. It seems fairly well established that under certain conditions punishment given for a poor performance often causes the learner to improve. However, punishment as the only type of treatment or as treatment in return for a good performance would obviously have an adverse effect.

6

An experiment was conducted concerning the use of *praise* and *reproof*. One group in a learning situation was given praise each day regardless of its performance. Another group was reproved each day regardless of its performance. A third group was given neither praise nor reproof. The result of this experiment was that the praised and reproved group performed about alike the first day. After that, the praised group showed steady improvement and the reproved group showed a gradual decrease in learning. The third group showed neither progress nor lack of progress. They continued with the same performance day after day.

Man is greatly stimulated to additional effort when he is *competing* with others. He understands that social recognition will come to those who achieve, who win and who are successful. This statement will hold true for the athlete, the business man and the housewife. However, it is equally true that overly intense rivalry can have a disruptive effect on performance. It can also have an adverse effect on learning.

While some unintentional learning occurs, to be lasting and effective learning must be motivated. People who are guided through performances in a mechanical manner instead of initiating their own responses do not achieve complete learning. Guidance will aid the learning process only when the learner has a clear intention to learn.

It is not clearly understood which kind of motivation works best for each individual. Praise is better than blame, but we do not know to what extent. Some rare individuals are motivated more by blame than by praise, and others even more by money than by either. However, the interested coach can draw some general conclusions which should be of value in giving instruction in motor skills.

Learning Conditions

Motivation in itself does not insure that the learning process will take place automatically. Certain other conditions must exist. Some of these conditions are more important than others, and none is sufficient when it stands alone. The most important of these conditions are *exercise, effect, knowledge of results, recency* and *intensity*.

Repetition of the learning situation usually helps in aiding learning to take place. Learning of skills on the basis of a single performance is quite rare. The more we repeat a certain response to a situation, the greater is the likelihood that the same response will occur in the same situation later. Further, in order to increase proficiency, we must repeatedly respond to the learning situation. *Passive* repetition, as we have already seen, does not lead to increased learning. The importance of *exercise* lies in the fact that it involves the repetition of *several* conditions which facilitate learning.

The *principle of effect* is supplementary to Thorndike's "Law of Exercise." It states, in general, that responses to a situation which satisfy the organism's needs tend to be retained, while those which fail to satisfy those needs tend to be eliminated. Another way to word this in coaching language is to say that situations which bring about positive or pleasant reactions tend to produce more learning. Situations which elicit negative or unhappy reactions cause less learning.

Motor skills are not developed unless the learner has a *knowledge of results*. Knowing the results of one's attempts leads to improvement through a tendency to repeat actions which were successful. We will usually correct some of the initial errors. There is also the element of the challenge to come closer to the target, to improve, to do better. Without the knowledge of how we are progressing, few of us would continue to put effort into any project.

The *intensity* of conditions associated with learning has influence upon the readiness to learn. Strong emotion will sometimes interfere with the efficient learning of complex skills. At times, however, emotion may lead to complete learning after only one response. For example, in situations which involve rivalry, a youngster launches himself fiercely into the task and may receive a more lasting response than after many practice efforts under different circumstances. We learn best those aspects of a situation which stand out vividly from others, such as those which are unique or novel.

All things being equal, *recent* experiences are more vivid. Therefore, the repetition of an act immediately or soon after the

first attempt usually gives better results than otherwise. The
validity of this statement is unchanged even though we must say
that there is evidence that many times the act performed earlier
is more vivid in the mind than the most recently performed act.
Moreover, first acts in a series tend to be more favorable for
learning.

Values of Different Learning Methods

What are the best procedures to be followed in developing
proficiency? Is it better to concentrate practice periods or to
distribute them with a longer interval between? Within a given
period of practice, is it better to make one attempt to learn and
act, or to repeat it often? What is the best amount of time to
allow between practice periods?

Investigation points to the fact that greater massing of trials,
in terms of trials to be learned, produces the *least economical*
type of learning—not, however, the *least learning.* Distributed
learning leads to greater gains than massed learning.

There are two problems concerned with distributed versus
massed effort. One is the optimal length of a particular practice
period, and the other is determination of the most economical
interval between practice periods of a given length. *Least economical* learning occurs with no interval between trials, and the
most economical interval is a one-day period. However, the advantage of the one-day interval is not far greater than that of a
one-minute interval. An advantage of distributed learning in a
particular situation is to help eliminate fatigue, which causes an
unhappy memory to be associated with the attempt. This could
cause resistance to later repetitions of the same act, thereby
producing poor learning.

A vast amount of research has gone into the matter of determining relative efficiency of the *part* and *whole* methods. The
part method allows the individual to concentrate on one portion
of the material, or one aspect of a skill, at a time. The *whole
method* calls for the individual to concentrate on the entire task.
The result of the research seems to run something like this: *parts*
are easier to learn and the learner is often *more happy* than when
confronted with the whole. He carries some of the skills and

knowledge over to the learning of the whole; however, he finds that putting the learned parts together is a serious problem requiring a great deal more work. If he can adjust himself to the whole method and handle it properly, he can learn better through this method. He may save time using the part method if he cannot adjust himself to the magnitude of the task presented by the whole method. It seems best to begin with the whole problem, with a willingness to concentrate at any time on a part which presents difficulty to the learner.

The Acquisition of Skills

Learning to withdraw a limb at a signal or developing positive or negative attitudes toward situations are hardly within the category of skilled performance. These are *conditioned responses* which are not complex enough to be called *skills*. *Skill,* as such, is proficiency in the performance of a task. Some psychologists prefer to differentiate between *verbal* and *motor* skills. As it is impossible to separate the two, we shall consider them together.

Skills are acquired only when the learner has a reason or a use for them. They are not acquired simply by the impingement of stimuli upon nerve receptors. The chief reason for acquisition of skill is inadequacy of the status quo. As long as the present situation satisfies every need, little change occurs.

Some skill is acquired through *trial and error.* Such hit or miss activity is not the best method, but it is one method. Sometimes this trial and error may be preceded by *insight,* which certainly increases the chances of quicker learning. Sometimes *implicit* trial and error precedes insight. This is a process of thinking out the various possible moves instead of actually making them. The least valuable type of trial and error is called *overt,* whereby the individual actually performs all the possible moves to determine the best one.

In acquiring complex physical skills one may use overt and implicit trial and error, or a combination of these two. If the learner has proper guidance, he will learn from the simple to the complex through oral instruction, demonstration and practice directed by another person.

The learner will learn some things through *imitation;* therefore, a demonstration is of great value. Imitation alone is not enough to teach complex skills, but it is of some benefit. Demonstration saves the learner time which might be wasted in trial and error. Observing a skilled performance as a learning technique may give the observer much insight into the skill which was acquired by the demonstrator only after a long, tedious process.

Some motor skills are developed partly through *memorization*. We tend to remember the acts which lead to the best results. We remember what we have observed another do in a like circumstance.

Levels of Complexity in Habit Formation

Most complex skills, such as those involved in playing a major sport like basketball, require an integration of simpler skills. They also involve successively higher stages of integration as learning proceeds.

One first learns to bounce and throw the ball. He then learns to make simple basketball shots. After a while, the relationship of these three movements begins to take shape in his mind. When simple skills of this nature are mastered, the player is ready to learn some of the finer skills of the game, such as tipping, rebounding and play making.

After complicated skills are practiced for a long time, they become automatic. This is called *habit formation*. It is the big reason why youngsters should learn the *correct* methods of playing first. Good habits enable a player to perform a skill automatically; his mind is left clear to think out solutions to defensive alignments with which he may be confronted.

Learning Plateaus

As we have already hinted, there will be periods when no apparent learning is taking place. The learner may seem to stay at the same level of efficiency for some time. This leveling-off process is called a *learning plateau*. It may be caused by a lack of stimuli or by a breakdown of the old ones. Integration of simpler habits into more complex ones takes time, and this may be what is occurring. A conflict between old and new habits may have arisen. Whatever the causes, learning plateaus, or the leveling off of

learning at certain points, are natural and should not promote
undue worry.

Transfer of Skills

Development of one skill will often influence the learning of
another. It may be a positive influence which promotes quicker
acquisition of the new skill. It may be negative, because of the
dissimilarity of the two skills, and may slow down the development of the new skill. This negative influence is called *habit
interference.* In athletics it brings up the age-old debate about
the relative merits of one sport or another as a foundation for
over-all athletic development.

Bilateral Transfer of Skills

A simple instance of positive transfer is to be found in the
evidence showing development of the right hand as the result of
skill acquired with the left hand, or vice versa. This is called
bilateral transfer or *cross-education.* The transfer may be from
hand to foot, foot to foot, or foot to hand. Where transfer occurs,
it involves similarity of techniques, similarity of principles or a
combination of these. An example is the quick learning of rebound
timing after having developed great proficiency at volleyball.
Another example is the learning of court tactics in tennis after
years of playing badminton.

Negative transfer can and does occur, so that we have *habit
interference.* It slows down the speed of the learner in acquiring
a new skill. This means that the techniques, skills and principles
of the learned skill are opposed entirely or in part to those of the
new skill. This is caused when we are called upon to make a new
approach to a situation to which we have already developed an
approach. For this reason, basketball players should be started
young and taught the correct procedures. It is the reason why a
skilled teen-age basketball player can learn to play football
quickly but the skilled football player may have great difficulty
in learning to play basketball.

Physiological Limits

Learning will approach a limit beyond which performance
cannot improve. The physiological limit is approached as the

individual gets to the point where he cannot manipulate any faster. He is like the miler whose legs cannot go any faster. Performance cannot rise above the point where performance is perfect.

Often the extremely skilled person fails to attain the potential of which he is capable. He performs sufficiently well to get by and stops there. To the average observer it seems that the player has reached his limit. Stiffer competition, higher rewards or enough incentive will lead him to increase his efficiency. His learning then continues, showing that his physiological limit had not been reached.

In summary, we can make certain broad generalizations for the benefit of basketball teachers. Start the player young and teach him the correct way the first time. In teaching him, allow him to imitate good demonstrations. Distribute the practice time to the best advantage. Motivate him, give him recognition and make the learning conditions as favorable as possible. Give him continual guidance in helping him see and know the results of his performances. Provide for his progress from the simple to the complex. Make the learning experience as pleasant as you can.

Part II

TEACHING OFFENSIVE SKILLS

3. Basket Shooting

Shooting baskets is the culmination of all offensive effort. In our efforts to impress players with the value of developing *all* fundamentals skills, we sometimes fail to place shooting in its proper perspective.

Shooters are made—not born. It is a great mistake to assume that all other fundamentals can be taught and to leave a player to develop his own scoring style. Some outstanding coaches have publicly stated that they never tamper with a boy's shooting form, especially if he is shooting well. This type of reasoning might cause Ben Hogan to continue a bad habit and shoot seventy-fives, when he could work on an error and shoot seventies. In other sports, we always assume that performance can be improved; yet in basketball we are superstitious and are reluctant to make a change in a player's style of shooting.

The time will come when any shooting percentage less than 50 per cent is ineffective. We should be changing or improving shooting styles just as we change or improve other skill performances. Therefore, the very first step that must be taken before giving shooting instructions is that the coach develop enough courage and faith to use a positive approach. The positive approach does not necessarily mean that one is to be dogmatic or narrowminded. It doesn't mean that the coach won't be able to adjust his pet styles to the various anatomical types with which he will deal. The positive approach means that he will not use words like "maybe" and "if." It means he will not be reluctant to change an unorthodox shooter if he deems it necessary.

Shooting is easily taught, for it is the one fundamental skill players will work on during their free time. It is easily taught because a player's interest automatically doubles when you begin talking about this fundamental. Therefore, he is more receptive and gives a more intense response to the instruction. Shooting is easily taught because it is a simple, mechanical movement that brings a great deal of pleasure to the performer.

To demonstrate to the learner how easy shooting can be, stand on a ladder and drop *two* basketballs through the basket at the same time. Two balls side by side will actually fit in the basket. The player should be encouraged to think about shooting in a confident manner. This little demonstration will help prove your point. Encourage the athletes to think of the *little* ball and the *big* basket. This psychological trick will increase confidence. The accurate shooter *believes* his shot is going in the basket. If he should miss, he *knows* he can put the next one in.

The shooter should be directed into orthodox shooting styles. The unorthodox shooter is generally a grandstand player. He is usually unorthodox in performing other fundamental skills. It is usually the unorthodox, behind-the-back passer who hurts you in the tight situations. He will declare that his contortions are habitual, that they are natural and that he just cannot perform any other way. If you will probe more deeply, you will find that the majority of his unorthodox wiggles are designed to please the crowd, and that he doesn't *want* to perform any other way. If you cannot effect an immediate compromise with this player, you will not be the coach; he will.

Good shooting requires poise, confidence and relaxation. We list all three of these traits because one is rarely found without the others. A perceptible physical and psychological change should come over the good player as he moves from defense to offense. He will change from the aggressive, jerky movements of the defensive player to the cool, calm, poised, unhurried movements of the offensive player. All of this spells relaxation. The tense player is a poor one to take the shot. The slang expression "Get loose" has been developed by the players themselves, and it points out their own knowledge that they shoot better when relaxed.

Balance is an outstanding quality of all great shooters. The unbalanced shooter is tense. He is a prayer shooter. He is a wishful thinker. In some instances, he is a grandstand player. Good balance comes from a controlled movement of the entire body. It results from not moving at a speed so fast that the performer cannot stop his dribble, take a pass, change directions or take a balanced shot. Most offensive players would have better balance on all offensive movements simply by *slowing down*. The offensive player should be encouraged to operate at a speed that he can *control*. Some players will be able to move more quickly than others and still stay under control. Control produces good shooting.

To teach shooting fundamentals effectively:

1. Use a positive, confident approach.
2. Demonstrate and explain why shooting is *easy*. Develop player confidence.
3. Direct players into orthodox shooting styles.
4. Impress each man with the importance of relaxation.
5. Require all players to shoot only when they are under control and on balance.

SECTION I: LAY-UP SHOOTING

Good lay-up shooting involves three major steps. For teaching purposes it is best to break the skill into several categories. These parts should be taught individually and then put together as a unit. It is best to analyze and demonstrate the entire skill of lay-up shooting before work is begun on the various component skills.

The Approach

The approach can be made with or without the ball. Most beginners find it easier to learn lay-up shooting without dribbling prior to the take-off. Therefore, we will give this method first consideration. The performer faces the basket at an angle of 45 degrees in relationship to the backboard. His distance from the goal should be about 25 feet. Righthanders start from the right side and lefthanders from the left side. If the performer has had no basketball experience, it is amazing how little difference it makes which hand is used first.

The coach stands directly in front of the basket in the keyhole area. The learner should make a jogging, controlled, straight approach to the basket for a pass from the coach and the subsequent lay-up.

The performer should receive a soft, easy pass as his right foot strikes the floor at a point which will allow him to take one more stride, plant the left foot and take off for the lay-up. He will watch the ball closely and be a good receiver by grasping the ball firmly. He will carry the ball with both hands to the right of his body and about waist high prior to the take-off.

A   B

ILLUSTRATION 1.   (A) *Receiving.*   (B) *Ball Shift.*

The Take-Off

After receiving the pass and shifting the ball, the shooter takes one more stride before leaping. This last stride should be longer than the initial steps. As the last stride is completed, the shooter's left foot is planted about one yard from the basket. The shooter's hips settle lower. The left knee bends considerably prior to the high kick with the right knee and leg. This action appears much like that of the good belly-roll high jumper.

The shooter will look up, focus his eyes at a point on the backboard about eight inches above and slightly to the right of the rim. The long last stride and foot plant creates a "braking" action which slows him down and allows time to get on balance for shooting. The shooter then lifts the right knee vigorously and strongly extends the left leg and ankle. He carries the ball high above the right shoulder with *both* hands in preparation for the shot.

ILLUSTRATION 2. (A) *Foot Plant.* (B) *High Jump.*

The Shot

At the peak of the player's jump and two-arm stretch, the performer stretches still higher by raising the right shoulder. When the right arm and shoulder are fully extended, the ball is softly propelled by the right hand and wrist. After being removed from the ball, the left hand and arm offer some protection from opponents' shot blocking efforts. The shooter will land almost directly under the basket. This means he must transfer his forward momentum upward in a high jump rather than forward in a broad jump action. The ball is released with no spin or a slight backspin, so that a *true* bounce will occur when it strikes the boards.

Most of the force applied in making the shot comes from the fingers and wrist. Since the ball is to be put up gently and the

ILLUSTRATION 3. *Lay Up.*

shooter is high in the air, little force is necessary. A full extension
of the fingers and flexion of the wrist will suffice.

Teaching Foot Plant, Take-Off and Shot

Here is a procedure that eliminates wrongfooted take-offs and
missed passes. It offers the satisfaction of achievement to beginners.

Station the beginner two yards from the basket at an angle
of 45 degrees with the backboard. He should stand with his feet
parallel. Let him start at this point with a basketball in his hands.
He will perform the foot plant by striding one full step forward
with his left foot. He performs the shot by carrying the ball high
with both arms and making the shot with his right hand. He
does not dribble the ball. All of this action appears as a one-stride
high jump.

After the beginner has mastered the one-stride lay-up, move
him back to the 25-foot distance. Let him attempt to jog in,
receive the pass and make the lay-up. It is possible that the

ILLUSTRATION 4. *Lay Up.*

beginner will have to go back time and time again to the one-stride lay-up.

Lay-ups should be practiced from both sides of the goal after initial instruction has been given.

Some common beginners' mistakes are:

1. Jumping off the wrong foot.
2. Putting "english" or spin on the ball.
3. Laying the ball against the board too hard.
4. Receiving the ball improperly.
5. Broad jumping.

It is necessary to watch each action carefully. Corrections must be made when they occur. Continual repetition and day-by-day drilling are mandatory. Every effort should be made to make shooting drills interesting and enjoyable. The instructor and learner must be constantly working and looking ahead to that time when the learner will have developed his skills well enough to be a varsity basketball player. Most veteran basketball coaches

can look at a college lay-up shooter and determine whether the
shooter received good instruction as a beginner.

SECTION 2: JUMP SHOOTING

It has been truthfully said many times that the jump shot has
brought about greater improvement in scoring than any other
basketball innovation. When performed well, it is virtually impossible to block. The shot has not yet been fully exploited. Players will be shooting it from greater distances each season. The
time will probably come when few players ever shoot a set shot.
The reason for this is very simple: players will be able to shoot
the jump from set shot distances; so the need for a set shot will
be eliminated.

When the jump shot first became popular, most youngsters
could shoot it accurately from around the free throw line. Shorter
distances caused them to "pull" it too much. Greater distance
caused them to strain too much for accuracy. Players are learning
to lessen the height of the jump for long distance shots and to
soften the impetus given the ball for short shots. Most modern
day college guards can jump shoot successfully from what is considered the regular guard spot. Most forwards in the single post
system can successfully shoot from the forward position. A
majority of ball clubs are striving to get inside to the jump shot
range anyway. They take most of their shots as jumps.

When the longer shot becomes necessary against a zone or
sagging man-to-man, the players have learned that, with less
emphasis on the jump, they can shoot a soft variation of the jump
shot. We will call this shot the "set jump shot," since it is usually
taken at what was once set shooting distance. Its techniques are
nearly the same as those for the jump shot, but there is enough
difference to warrant explanation. This "set jump shot," or jump
shot from greater distance, is causing defenses great harassment.
By adding this shot to their repertoire, many players now shoot
all shots using nearly the same muscles and movements. The
free throw one-hander is most popular. The one-handed lay-up,
jump shot and set jump shot are all similar in movement. This
specialization of motion must of necessity bring greater efficiency.

A. The Moving Jump Shot

The jump shot is somewhat different when performed after a cutting or dribbling drive. It becomes necessary to stop forward momentum and transfer it upward. It requires catching the ball successfully and coming to a halt without improper footwork, in the case of the cutter. Jump shooters have been successful by placing the right foot always slightly ahead, by placing the left foot always ahead and by placing the feet parallel and shoulder width apart. The best balance and braking action are obtained by the last method. If one foot should be advanced only slightly, however, the shot will not be affected greatly.

ILLUSTRATION 5.   *Foot Alignment for Jump Shot.*

After the shooter has braked forward momentum and gathered in the ball, he must adjust it quickly in his hands for the shot. Grasping the ball and adjusting the hands for the shot should be performed simultaneously. For the righthanded shooter, this means placement of both hands on the ball so that, when the arms are raised, the right hand will be behind the ball and the left hand will be on the bottom left. The left hand will not be directly under the ball nor directly to the left side but at a compromise point between those two positions. The fingers of both hands will be spread, with the spread of the shooting hand slightly exaggerated. The shooting hand needs to be as widely spread as is comfortable. The palm of neither hand should touch the ball. The right hand should be flexed or tense, so that the fingers are barely "gripping" the ball. A slight gripping causes the shooter to "feel" the ball and shoot with a full extension of his wrist and fingers instead of shoving it or shooting with a limp wrist. A firm grasp should be maintained until the actual shot begins.

The jump shooter should brake action and gather in the ball simultaneously. He then gets on balance for an upward jump.

ILLUSTRATION 6. *Position of Hands.*

If he is cutting to his left or right, the tendency is for him to float sideways. If he is moving toward the goal, he will tend to float forward. He should fight this natural tendency by learning to get on balance and jump upward after coming to a halt from any cutting angle. No harm is actually done if the jumper travels *forward* in the air a distance of 12 to 15 inches, provided there is no defensive man near that he could possibly travel into.

If the defensive man is near, the shooter must go straight up and come down as straight as he possibly can. Most boys have to fight a tendency to travel backward when the defensive man is near. They should curb this tendency, for they usually take their shot with them when they fall away. If the ball goes in one direction and the shooter in another direction, there is poor economy of motion. The shooter should therefore strive to use forward momentum and extension of arm, hand and wrist to produce an *economy of motion* that results in a relaxed shooting style.

The jump should be made from flexed legs. The strongest jumps are not made from straight legs. If the crouch or leg flexion is *too* great, it delays the jumper. The sooner the jumper gets into the air, the easier time he will have in getting his shot off unguarded. However, he should take time to get an adequate leg bend for a good, strong, high jump shot.

The jumper should have his eyes on the target—the *entire* target—the bull's-eye. He should not sight on the rim, front or back. He should be concentrating on the whole circle of the basket, mentally picturing it as a bull's-eye.

Many good players sight for the front rim. That is, they try to drop the ball just over a point on the front of the rim. Some

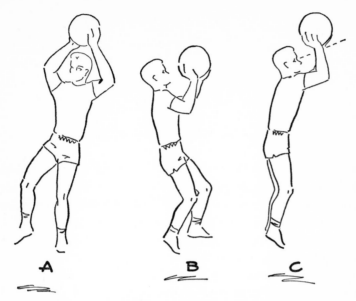

ILLUSTRATION 7. *(A) Sideward Motion. (B) Backward Motion.*
(C) Balanced Jumper.

ILLUSTRATION 8. *Good Leg Flexion.*

great coaches teach this method. Nevertheless, we believe it is
best to aim at what you intend to hit—the basket.

The jumper leaves the floor with a powerful spring caused by
a full extension of the legs, ankles and feet. If he is properly
balanced, he will be traveling straight upward. When he has

ILLUSTRATION 9. *(A) Poor Sight Picture. (B) Good Sight Picture.*

reached the peak of his jump, he will "hang" or balance very briefly for the shot. Many shooters exaggerate this "hanging" in the air and have their shots blocked. The shot should not be taken while the performer is still moving upward; nor should it be taken while he is moving back down. If the shooter balances too long in the air, he will find that he is actually releasing the ball while returning to the floor.

This hanging or balancing can be accomplished in two ways. One is to lift the knees slightly, thus creating a rudder action against further altitude and a balancing action. The other method is to stiffen the legs momentarily when good height has been obtained. The leg stiffening method seems to enable the shooter to get his shot off faster and get just as much balance. Therefore, this is the method that is recommended. When the leg flexing system is used, shooters should be cautioned against over-flexion.

As the jump begins, the ball should be started on its way to shooting position. Shooting position should be obtained simultaneously with the balancing action. In bringing the ball to shooting position, the player should keep the ball close to the body all the time. If the ball is swung out and back to position, opposing forces of motion are created, causing a loss of power. By keeping the ball close during the upward body thrust, the player can make the shot as one continuous motion upward and out, with the exception of the brief balancing action where the ball is "locked" into shot position. A "freezing" motion requires only a split second but is necessary in order to keep the shooter from utilizing too much of the upward momentum created by the jump. If too much of the upward momentum is used, the shot will usually be too strong. A minimum amount of the upward thrust

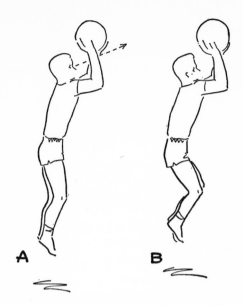

ILLUSTRATION 10. *(A) Straight-Legged Method.*
(B) Bent-Legged Method.

is still very properly used in the actual shot, creating an effort-less hand and wrist shot.

The ball is frozen into shooting position at the same time that the legs are bent or stiffened. It will be supported primarily by the left hand. The ball is above eye level; sighting takes place from underneath. The right arm, from elbow to shoulder girdle,

ILLUSTRATION 11. *(A) Position of Ball in Relation to Body During Jump.*

should be parallel to the floor. The left arm is inclined slightly backward so that the ball is held with its back portion touching an imaginary line drawn straight upward from the forehead. The shooter should keep his shoulders squared away with the goal. Neither shoulder is advanced. This enables him to shoot equally well whether driving to his right or left. He should relax during the shot. Relaxation is difficult to master, since the jump is fairly strenuous.

ILLUSTRATION 12.   *Ball in Relation to Head, Arms and Shoulders.*

The shooter must relax during his shooting motion. The actual shot is the simplest part of the whole action, if all the other movements have been correctly executed. It is made by a full extension of the shooting arm and a full extension of the shooting fingers and wrist. The ball leaves the index and middle fingers last. The left hand comes off naturally just after extension of the shooting arm begins. The left hand and arm are allowed to pull back naturally toward the shooter's left chest, causing ease of follow-through. The shooting shoulder will begin to ride slightly forward when the shot is made.

If correct action has been used, the shooter will land on balance. In many cases he will be able to rebound his own shot. However, all concentration and thought during the shot should be on the bull's eye. The shooter should even follow through mentally to make sure he is concentrating fully. He can almost "think" the ball into the target if he concentrates while applying proper physical action.

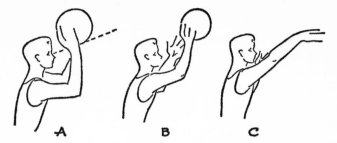

ILLUSTRATION 13. *(A) Start of Shot. (B) Left Hand Leaves Ball.*
(C) Follow-Through.

B. The Standing Jump Shot

The standing jump is more difficult than the moving jump shot. Little forward momentum can be generated or used. Therefore, more attention is given to the actual jump. The result of the standing jump shot depends on the leg strength and quickness of the individual.

Some forward momentum can be gained by sliding the right foot (for the right hander) forward as the shooter goes into his crouch. If the shooter couples his foot slide with a *quick* crouch and jump, he will be able to make the jump with greater ease. His right foot is forward and there is a lateral separation of the feet of about 12 inches. Total weight is distributed evenly on *both* feet.

ILLUSTRATION 14. *Foot Slide.*

The foot slide and crouch are executed as one movement. A low crouch is helpful because the height of the jump is more dependent on the legs than in the moving jump. The crouch and foot slide should not delay the shooter. A *quick* jump is as important as a *high* jump. Slow jumpers will experience trouble in getting their shots off, even though they may be able to jump exceptionally high.

All other shooting action is the same as that described for the moving jump shot.

ILLUSTRATION 15.   *Foot Slide and Crouch.*

C. The Set Jump Shot

There was a time when high school coaches did not allow their players to shoot the jump shot. They assumed it was too difficult or better suited to college basketball. Even those coaches who did come to use it restricted their players to *short* jump shots. Meanwhile, college and professional players were shooting the jump from greater and greater distances.

The progress of basketball has been speeded up many times by players who performed experimental shots or movements that may have, at the time, created grave doubt in the minds of their coaches. Sometimes these experiments were encouraged and sometimes they were discouraged. The fact remains that many of the techniques that we teach assiduously today were used long before they were considered standard or proved to the point that coaches actually spent part of the practice period teaching them.

While few coaches are teaching the jump shot as a long shot, many players are using it successfully thus, in place of the set shot. It would appear that the logical move is to begin teaching it, so that even greater improvement can be made in its performance.

The set jump shot can be used most effectively by cutting down on the height of the jump. If the shot is a culmination of movement, either a cutting maneuver or a dribble, slightly more height can be used. Greater distance from the goal should cause the jumper to realize that a strenuous jump will not leave him with enough power for the shot. Therefore, the height of the jump will depend on the distance from the goal. We will discuss a shot taken from about one yard from the head of the circle. This is a distance of about 30 feet.

If the shooter is standing still, he may utilize a short foot slide. A moderate crouch is all that is necessary. Speed in getting the shot off is still essential. The shooter will not bring the ball as high as he normally would in shooting a close-in, strong high jumper. He should bring it to a point high enough to sight *under* the ball, however.

Little or no "hanging" motion is needed. The shooter simply takes a slight jump of eight or ten inches and shoots the ball as soon as he is in the air. It will give the illusion that he is releasing the ball on the way upward. Actually, he is taking only a low jump and releasing as soon as he achieves the height of the jump.

ILLUSTRATION 16. *The Set Jump Shot.*

The lack of arm extension overhead creates a "cocking" angle of the shooting arm. This gives more arm, hand, finger and wrist strength. The eyes should be glued on the target and all other jump shooting techniques should be utilized.

SALIENT TEACHING POINTS FOR JUMP SHOTS

1. When moving for the shot, come to a balanced halt.
2. Jump from both feet.
3. Make the jump *straight* up.
4. Carry the ball up to position, keeping it close to the body.
5. The shooting hand should be *directly* behind the ball.
6. Some crouch is necessary for good height.
7. Take a concentrated sight picture.
8. Sight from under the ball.
9. Freeze the ball at the shooting position.
10. Relaxation is needed for the shot.
11. Follow through is necessary, just as in the free throw or set.
12. Teach the standing, moving and set jump shots separately.

SECTION 3: SET SHOOTING

There are as many different styles of set shooting as there are basketball players. The ever increasing importance of the jump shot, however, makes it desirable for the set shot to correspond as closely as possible in form and technique with the jump shot. With this view in mind, we shall discuss and illustrate here the one-hand push shot. The jump shot is actually no more than the one-hand push executed while in the air. Therefore, all work directed toward the one-hander will have a good transfer value to the jump shot.

A. The One-Hand Push Shot

Stance. The stance for the best one-hand push will cause the shooter to place both feet solidly on the floor. The right foot will be advanced to at least a heel and toe alignment and possibly more. The feet will be spread from three to eight inches from right to left. Many one-handed shooters take a short step, a rock step or various other "crow hopping" actions, all of which take needless time and effort. The simplest, easiest, quickest one-hander is the balanced flat-footed push. The knees will be flexed as the shot begins.

ILLUSTRATION 17.   *Stance for Push Shot.*

Ball Grasp.   Hand position on the ball is precisely the same as for the jump shot. The right hand is spread, fingers grip slightly, and the palm is off the ball. The left hand is supporting the ball on the bottom left.

ILLUSTRATION 18.   *Grasp.*

Arm Position

The ball is held at eye level so that the shooter sights directly over it. It is held in front of the head at a distance that leaves the forearm at a ninety degree angle or almost perpendicular to the floor. The upper arm will be parallel to the floor. The left arm is relaxed and carries the greater weight of the ball. The ball should be placed on a line between the shooter's right eye and the basket.

The Shot. The shot begins with a moderate knee dip. The ball is drawn closer to the shooter's face and dropped to about chin level. This motion creates a cocking of the legs, wrists and elbows. The ball moves in one continuous motion as the shot is made by extending the legs, ankles, right elbow, wrist and fingers. The arc of the ball and its release will describe a small U shape. The movement is a circular, rhythmic, continuous motion coupled with the action of the legs and ankles. The ball leaves the index finger and the middle finger at the same time. The fingers and wrist should be strongly flexed at the time the ball is released. All vision should be focused intently on the target and the shooter should concentrate. The follow through results in the shooter rising up on the toes with a full extension of the ankles. The shooter may possibly leave the floor momentarily. Force is applied by *both* legs. As the right arm is extended, the right shoulder follows. The left hand comes off the ball and the left shoulder is pulled slightly to the rear. The arm should be straightened fully in the follow through, with the wrist bent downward in an exaggeratedly flexed position.

A   B   C   D

ILLUSTRATION 19. *The Sequence of the One-Hand Push Shot.*

The Two-Hand Set Shot

The two-hand set shot is highly regarded by many coaches. In certain parts of the country, players have developed an area pride in their ability to shoot the two-hander. They shoot it so well that those of us who may not normally teach the two-hander often wonder why we don't.

The two-hander usually requires a little more time to deliver. Strong defensive teams cause the shooter to get his shot off quickly; therefore, such teams will lessen the effectiveness of the average two-hand shooter. While some youngsters learn to get it off amazingly fast, percentages are against the average player achieving a great deal of speed in delivery. The two-hand set is good against a zone or against sinking man-for-man defenses.

Some boys are apparently too small or too weak to employ the jump shot with great effectiveness. Such players may well develop the two-hand set to a high degree and become just as dangerous on offense as the naturally stronger boy with the good jump.

Foot Position. Position of the feet may vary according to the height and build of the individual boy. The average boy will get better results by placing his weight evenly on both feet and having them lined up parallel. They should be spread twelve to fifteen inches, depending upon the boy's size. By placing his feet side by side, the player leaves himself the opportunity to drive to his right or left if the defensive player crowds him too much to shoot. If he advances one foot, he is left the option only of driving in the direction of the foot that is advanced. Yet, you may find some boys who can get better balance by advancing one foot.

Ball Position. The ball should be held at face level, slightly below the eyes. This position causes the defensive man to stand very close if he wants to prevent the shot. If he crowds too much, he leaves the driving opportunity. The fingers of both hands should be spread well with the thumbs pointing diagonally inward toward the middle. The elbows should be held comfortably in, close to the sides. They should not be allowed to point outward as if the shooter were preparing to fly. They should not be forced

ILLUSTRATION 20. *(A) Balanced Foot Position.*

(B) Staggered Foot Position.

to an unnatural position. The elbows will be slightly wider than the body. The ball should be held about eight to ten inches in front of the face.

ILLUSTRATION 21. *2-Hand Set Shot: Ball Position, Side.*

The Shot. The shooter's eyes should be fixed on the *whole* target. He should bend the knees slightly and start the ball goalward with a very small arc motion. To execute this arc motion, the shooter will drop and pull the ball toward him. He will continue the motion upward and continue right into the shooting motion. This rhythmic motion is coupled with a flexing of the legs. As the thrusting action of the shot occurs, the legs and ankles are extended fully. The shooter extends the arms fully, allowing the hands to rotate naturally so that the palms are turned outward. He will rise up on his toes during the follow through; if he actually leaves the floor, no harm is done, unless it is an extreme unbalancing action. The ball is kept high at all times. The eyes are focused intently on the target. The shot is made rhythmically and is one continuous action. The legs, ankles and arms are extended fully.

ILLUSTRATION 22. (A) *Starting Position.* (B) *Flexion.* (C) *Extension.*

The Hook Shot

The hook shot is probably the hardest shot to teach. It is also one of the least used shots today. Rarely does any basketball player, other than the pivot or center, use it. This leaves the coach with the task of teaching one, two or three men this particular shot. While some coaches teach this shot to every boy on the squad, it is generally agreed that its greatest value is gained by use in the pivot area. It is a rather hard shot to learn. Youngsters like to try it, they like to shoot it; yet, from a physiological standpoint, it requires an unusually great amount of work and repetition to shoot this shot well.

Starting Position. Normally, the hook shot is made from a starting position with the back to the goal. This is the main reason most teams teach it only to their pivot men. Let us assume that the pivot man is standing just outside the key hole area on the right side of the goal, and two yards closer to the goal than the free throw line. He will step almost straight toward the baseline, pointing his left foot down the side of the key hole area. By stepping down the key hole line he comes much closer to the goal for the shot than he would otherwise do. Beginners should be discouraged from stepping away from the goal.

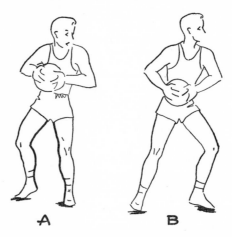

ILLUSTRATION 23.   *(A) Starting Position.   (B) First Step.*

The Shot. After planting the left foot, the shooter will start the ball upward and sideward so that his right arm will ultimately pass in front of his chest. The shooting arm is slightly flexed and curled behind the ball. The left hand is kept on the ball until the natural time for the ball to be released, when it will come off and the shooting arm will be extended even more. The head is turned in toward the basket so that the shooter can get full benefit of his entire vision. The chest is turned toward the goal during the follow through, this giving the shooter even more reason for stepping toward the basket instead of away from it. The right arm is straightened fully just before the ball is released. The fingers are flexed as the ball leaves the shooting hand. The left arm acts as a protective barrier against the defensive man. The left leg is fully extended and may leave the floor briefly. The right leg is lifted with the shot.

ILLUSTRATION 24. *(A) Carry Position. (B) Delivery.
(C) Follow Through.*

The Free Throw

All coaches realize the value of shooting free throws well. They realize that these points represent as high as 50 per cent of total point production on occasion. Yet, we rarely hear a discussion of free throwing at clinics or during informal coaches' talking sessions. Offensive patterns, game strategy and the more tactical aspects of the game seem to command greater interest. When we look at our shot charts at the end of a game or the end of a season, we find that nearly half of our points did not come from any of these parts of the game. They came from our ability or lack of ability at the free throw line.

During the 1958-1959 season at Oglethorpe University, 24 games were won and one lost. Oglethorpe scored 519 field goals for a total of 1,036 points. The field goal shooting percentage was

43.5%. 427 points were scored from the free throw line for a shooting percentage of 65.9%. This means that .291 of our total point production came from the free throw line. It is highly probable that Oglethorpe did not spend as much as five per cent of its total practice time at the free throw line; yet, it achieved 30 per cent of its results there. These figures are offered here as a concrete example of the importance of free throwing to a team's success.

It would be well to take considerable time to emphasize such facts to the team so that they too will understand the importance of shooting free throws. They should understand that the reliable free throwers will receive more than average consideration when the coach selects his starting five. Surely an award of some sort should be presented to the best percentage free thrower at the end of the season.

Techniques for All Free Throwers

Varying styles of shooting free throws will cause coaches to offer a great deal of individual instruction during the teaching of this shot. However, there are several basic techniques that should be employed by all shooters, regardless of style.

Relaxation is *essential*. Some free throwers who seem not to be able to miss during practice do not shoot a respectable game time percentage. They are mechanically sound, physiologically correct, and they concentrate intently. Yet they do not make the game time free throw often enough. Such players have not learned to relax. They allow game time distractions or other factors to cause them to tighten their muscles. Tensing of the muscles causes a shooter to shoot an entirely different shot than the one he has practiced. It also causes the shooter to miss the shot.

How do we get the players to relax? Several methods have been used successfully. The professionals take a deep breath and/or bounce the ball several times before shooting. Remember that the shooter has ten seconds to get his shot off. Some players have tried dangling the arms limply for two or three seconds. Any procedure that will bring the shooter to a relaxed state is desirable.

Concentration is *essential*. The successful free thrower cannot be thinking about his girl friend in the stands. He cannot be worried about next week's algebra test. He must have every ounce of physical and mental concentration on the task at hand. Crowd noises should be closed from his mind.

Aiming is *essential*. Sighting for the free throw should be the same as for the set or jump shots. It should consist of the *whole* target. As it was mentioned earlier, shooters might benefit by assuming mentally that the goal is a bull's-eye. They should not aim for the front or back of the rim. They should look and aim at the entire target, so that it can be centered. The shooter should aim at what he wants to hit; few players want to hit the front or the back of the rim.

A good *follow through* is *essential*. No matter what type shot is used, the follow through is necessary. It consists of a full extension of all limbs brought into use during the particular motion employed. Jerking the hands off the ball or stopping motion at the point of ball release will cause the shot to be faulty. A good follow through will give the shooter relaxation and thereby improve his concentration. A good follow through causes the shot to be "soft."

Confidence is *essential*. There is no way the shooter can become confident other than to become proficient. Make him aware of the ball as a *small* object and the goal as a *large* target. Encourage him to shoot practice shots until he *knows* he can hit the free throw. Some good practice shooters may become only average game shooters, but there are no poor practice shooters who are excellent game shooters. The best way to develop confidence is to practice correctly every day.

The One-Hand Free Throw

It is recommended that the free thrower shoot his free throw shot nearly like that of his set shot or jump shot. The one-hand push type free throw seems to correspond closely to the other shots that are employed during the normal course of basketball. Nevertheless, the value of the two-hand underhand method cannot be underrated. It has many merits, even though it employs a motion not used anywhere during the game except at the free throw line. Because the two-hand underhand method has been used so successfully by players at all levels, and because the one-hand push corresponds so closely to other shooting styles, we are going to analyze and suggest these two styles as the best for teaching purposes. If a player has a good two-hand set shot, there is no reason why he should not be allowed to use that method. If the learner is an elementary student and has no style, the following one-hand method is offered.

Stance. If the shooter is righthanded, his right toe should be placed close to the line and pointed straight toward the goal. His left foot will be placed two to five inches to the left and behind the right foot so that the toe of the left is on line with the heel of the right foot. The left foot may be pointed slightly to the left, creating an angle of about 15 degrees between the feet. A slight angling of the left foot allows the shooter to follow through better, since his right shoulder is going to ride forward with the shot. Body weight should be evenly distributed on both feet.

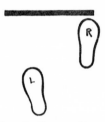

ILLUSTRATION. 25.   *Ordinary Free Throw: Stance.*

Ball Position. The ball is held just below eye level and about ten or twelve inches in front of the right eye. The fingers of the right hand are behind the ball so that the interval between the forefinger and index finger is centered on the ball. This means that the thumb and forefinger will be to the left or center and that the other three fingers are to the right of center. The left hand supports the weight of the ball and it is placed at the bottom left position. The palm of the right hand is not touching the ball and the fingers should be "feeling" or gripping slightly.

The Shot. The shot is executed much like that of the one-hand push, except that the feet cannot leave the floor. The ball is brought down and toward the chin to begin the shot. It continues in one motion upward and outward for the shooting motion.

ILLUSTRATION 26. *Ordinary Free Throw: Ball Position, Front.*

The shot motion thus becomes that of a small U arc. This arc motion gives rhythm to the shot. As the downward motion begins, the knees are flexed slightly. As the arc is completed, the knees, ankles, arm and wrist are extended completely for the follow-through. The left hand comes off as the right shoulder rides forward with the extension of the right arm. The left hand and arm are brought naturally back to the left chest. The line of motion should be *straight,* after it is initiated. Do not allow the shooter to start the ball at the center of his chest and release it on a line outside that of his shoulders. He should not hesitate or halt his motion when he draws the ball backward for the shot. A continuous motion is necessary.

ILLUSTRATION 27. (A) *Start.* (B) *Knee-Dip.* (C) *Ball Release.* (D) *Follow Through.*

The Two-Hand Underhand Shot

The two-hand underhand shot is as old as the game of basket-ball. It has successfully endured the test of time. Originally play-ers used this method to score field goals. Gradually it fell by the wayside as a field goal technique, because it was so easy to block. Since the shooter is not worried about getting his free shot blocked from the free throw line, the underhand method may be the best method for many players.

Some coaches insist that every member of their team shoot his free throws in this manner. I have not yet seen a team follow this rule with poor results. Observation of the good results these teams get causes us to put the underhand method in this basic manual as one of the two basic teaching techniques. The players should not be allowed to jump from one style to another in-discriminately. They should adopt a shot and stick with it. In some cases the coach will decide which shot is best.

Stance.   The feet should be placed about shoulder width apart and side by side. The feet should point straight ahead and the weight of the entire body should be placed evenly on both feet.

ILLUSTRATION 28.

Ball Position.   The ball is held at comfortable arm's length. The arms should be relaxed. Both hands grasp the ball with an even amount of grip. The fingers and thumbs hold the ball securely but not tightly. The palms are off the ball. The index finger of each hand should center the ball precisely in the middle of the seam that runs at either end of the ball. Shooters should always catch the ball so that the seams run horizontally to the floor. They are thus able to make use of a built-in advantage— the seams at either end. The thumbs will rest on top of the ball, pointing diagonally toward each other so that they form about a 45 degree angle. The arms are relaxed and extended so that the ball rests comfortably between the shooter's upper legs. The legs are straight during this starting position.

ILLUSTRATION 29.

The Shot. The shooter's eyes are focused intently on the target. He starts the shot by flexing the knees and allowing the ball to drop even lower. He keeps the upper trunk erect with little or no bending over from the waist. After a knee dip of about eight to ten inches, the shooter starts his shooting motion by swinging his arms out and upward. He should keep his arms straight all the way, with the thumbs and knuckles of the forefinger leading slightly. The arms and legs should be extended at the same time. When both arms and legs are extended, the ball leaves the shooter's hands softly, with as little spin as possible. A lack of spin gives the ball ample opportunity to drop in, even if it should strike the front or back rim. The shooter follows through by rising on his toes and raising his arms above his head with the palms down and thumbs rotated inward. He should concentrate on giving equal force to the shot with each hand.

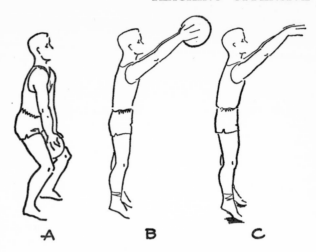

ILLUSTRATION 30.   (A) *Knee Dip.*   (B) *Shot.*
(C) *Follow Through.*

SUMMARY OF FREE THROW TEACHING STEPS

Make sure that the individual team members realize the importance of good free throwing to over-all success. Drills of varying types should be used and should resemble game conditions as closely as possible. No matter what type shot is used, the following conditions should exist:

1. Relaxation.
2. Concentration.
3. Aiming for the whole target.
4. Good follow through.
5. Confidence through practice.
6. Insistence that players not jump from one style to another.

COACHES' TEACHING HINTS

1. Have courage to make style changes that are fundamentally necessary.
2. Allow for differences in physique, but teach orthodox, balanced shooting.
3. Remember that concentration is essential for an effective shooting drill.

4. The sight picture should consist of the *whole* target—the basket.
5. Jump shooters should jump *straight* up instead of sidewards or backwards.
6. A good follow through is good insurance.
7. The shooter must *believe* he can hit the basket.

4. Passing and Receiving

Passing and receiving will be discussed at the same time so that each will assume the same degree of importance. Good passers without good receivers will have little opportunity to display their skill.

All the new basketball offenses have enhanced the value and importance of the passing game. The new pattern continuities require passers and receivers to be more adept. In many instances, the success of the pattern depends on completion of a particular pass. Some teams try to build their entire offense around the passing game, eliminating almost completely the dribble. Such teams develop sure, accurate passers and receivers because of the increased number of passes involved.

Good passers—or those who regularly lead in assists—possess one outstanding trait. They are basically and inherently *unselfish*. They are team conscious. They get a strong sense of satisfaction from setting a teammate up for a basket. It seems likely that good passers must also have above-average intelligence. The good passer in a free lance game should make a good chess player, because finding and hitting open men at strategic spots requires expert mental gymnastics.

A coach can do little about innate intelligence of individual team members. He can help a great deal in developing unselfishness. An award at season's end for the leader in "assists" will make a team pass conscious. All coaches should strive to make the outstanding passer receive as much recognition as outstanding shooters or rebounders. The coach can develop an offense that almost eliminates selfish temptation, because of a necessity for moving the ball to a certain place at a certain time.

Strong wrists, fingers and forearms are of utmost importance to the outstanding passer or receiver. Fingertip push-ups have proved to be excellent for physical development. Squeezing a small sponge ball daily during the off season is valuable and might be a supplementary exercise to the fingertip push-ups.

Peripheral or split vision has become increasingly important over the years. Unfortunately, some young players mistake blind passing for split vision passing. The coach should impress each man with the poor percentages involved in blind passing. He should also impress his players with the importance of not telegraphing the direction and time of an impending pass. Using split vision successfully requires only a *slight* turn of the head so that the passer does not look directly at the receiver. Some great players can see a range of more than 180 degrees. Each player must discover that range at which he can pass successfully. Each player can improve his split vision by simply practicing it during his day-to-day routine actions. He can practice split vision in the classroom, walking down the street or while eating. The coach must do a selling job in order to make each player aware of the importance of split vision and to get individually initiated action.

Finally, the coach must make each team member aware of his *responsibility* to pass effectively. Keeping account of each bad pass, you will find that a majority of ball losses are caused by poor passing or poor receiving. When a pass is not completed, the passer should ask himself why he failed. The receiver should ask himself the same question. Neither can be blamed as individuals; both must accept the responsibility for loss of the ball.

There are an unusually large number of passes that can be used successfully in various circumstances. Should the coach teach every single pass? Most of us have attempted this herculean task at one time or another. It is very doubtful if such a task can be performed by the most capable basketball teacher. Yet, while we do not attempt to teach every type of shot to each player, most of us try to practice every single type of pass. The boy is unusual who can effectively use more than three different passing techniques. It is highly probable that learning well three types of passes would bring more success than the half-learning of all types. Each coach should study his particular offense. He should then select the passes that are needed to make it "go." These passes should receive special attention at each practice session.

We will treat first the three passes that are more universally used and accepted. They are the bounce pass, the two-hand overhead pass and the two-hand chest pass. Other types that benefit various teams, depending upon their style of play, are the baseball pass, the hook pass, the sideward hook, the two-hand underhand pass, and the one-hand push pass.

The Bounce Pass

Left to his own devices, a novice will soon learn that this pass is very difficult to intercept. The average boy has an instinctive or reflexive desire to prevent an opponent from throwing the ball over his head. He will naturally hold his arms up to keep this from happening. His arms are hinged and attached at the shoulders. If he is six feet tall his hands and fingers are going to be too far from the floor to break up a moderately well-executed bounce pass. The bounce pass is simple. It is not spectacular. It is a good, basic, consistent, fundamentally sound method of moving the ball from one man to another. It is not unusually fast. The bounce pass should be used normally for short passing. Pattern teams will find its use advantageous. It is especially useful in attacking a zone defense.

Starting Position. Hold the ball belt high or lower. In order for the receiver to receive the ball well, it should be bounced up to his belt. If the pass is started lower or higher than its intended terminal height, completion becomes more difficult. For this reason, short players have found the bounce pass to be well adapted to their stature. They have found they can keep the ball low and bounce it under their taller opponents more successfully than they can hold it high and pass around the tall boys. The passer should be a potential driver if he has not already dribbled. He will advance one foot to cause the defensive man some anxiety as to whether he is to be a driver or a passer. Advancing the foot also brings him naturally to a lower position. If the defensive man doesn't have his arms high enough, the passer may fake a shot or high pass to cause him to bring them up. Of course, if the defensive man refuses to bring his arms up, the passer may always pass overhead.

The ball should be held securely in both hands. After a player has mastered the two-hand bounce pass, he is ready to learn the one-hand bounce pass. He should learn first with both hands.

ILLUSTRATION 31. *Bounce Pass, Start.*

The Pass. After the passer is sure his opponent's hands are high enough, he quickly passes the ball under the opponent's arms, causing the ball to strike the floor about midway between himself and his intended receiver. The ball should be passed with as little "spin" or rotation as possible. A spinning ball is hard to catch. Each passer should throw the ball in just the same manner that he likes to receive one. The passer needs little or no follow through. A follow through tells an opponent where the ball has gone. Concentrating on a follow through will sometimes tell an opponent where the ball is *going*, as it may cause the passer to *telegraph*. Telegraphing eliminates all the advantages gained by developing split vision. The passer should *see* his receiver clearly. To see him clearly does not necessarily mean that he has to look *directly* at him, thereby telling everybody on the floor his plans. The more advanced performer will find it helpful to look directly at the opponent he is attempting to pass by.

Passes should be snapped off with as little drawback motion as possible. A snap motion will get the ball off before defensive men can react. It will eliminate telegraphing to some extent. Passes should be made at brisk speed, but they should not be too hard to cach.

ILLUSTRATION 32. *Bounce Pass by Opponent,*
Indicates Height of Pass.

One-Hand Bounce Pass

After gaining effective use of a two-hand bounce pass, the learner is ready to adapt it to use by one hand in certain instances. Whenever the ball is handled with two hands, there is greater surety of action. Nevertheless, there are times when it is a distinct advantage to be able to use one hand while making the bounce pass.

There will be times when a receiver and passer are directly on line with a defensive man. At such times the passer may step slightly to one side or the other and make the bounce pass with one hand. Place the hand directly behind the ball to help in eliminating spin. There is also a tendency to pass too low when using only one hand. This tendency should be avoided. The passer should make his step and begin his pass all in one motion. If the one-hand bounce pass is to be used with complete effectiveness, it must be used equally well by right or left hands. That is one of the reasons it should not be attempted until the two-hand pass is well learned.

Note that the step out is taken with the right foot when the pass is made with the right hand. The pass can be made with a cross-over step. However, the next step is for the player to learn a fake pass and drive, and it is executed more easily if the step out is made with the foot that is on the same side as the passing hand.

ILLUSTRATION 33. *One-Hand Pass.*

The Two-Hand Overhead Pass

Here is another pass used a great deal by pattern teams. It is gaining in popularity more than any other pass because of its widespread use among the professional teams.

The two-hand overhead pass has one advantage over any other pass, especially for the tall player. It draws defensive men close enough to drive around. If they do not draw forward, the pass can be made with complete ease. This pass can be made without any giveaway motion; thus it is extremely difficult to block. It is a good feed pass to cutters or side post men, and it is a pass that all tall men should develop.

Starting Position.   The ball is raised overhead by both hands so that there is some flexion of the elbows. One foot should be advanced and both legs slightly flexed. This position is an excellent one from which to drive. If the passer is not harassed at all, he may straighten his legs. If he is crowded, he should bend the legs more and foot-fake, to keep the defensive man back far enough so that he will be unable to prevent the pass.

The Pass.   The ball should be passed to the receiver's shoulders. If it is passed at a lower point, it will be traveling at an

ILLUSTRATION 34. *Overhead Pass, Start.*

angle that would make it difficult to catch. Since it is started at a height greater than shoulder level, it will still be traveling somewhat downward. The passer will be tempted to pass too hard. He has both hands in use and gravity will be helping him. He should take into consideration direction of movement by the receiver and his height. Some passers look good until they have to hit a moving target. One of the most difficult passing techniques to master is passing to a receiver moving straight toward you. There is a strong tendency to pass too hard in this situation.

The two-hand overhead pass should be snapped off quickly and softly from the starting position, without any drawback of

ILLUSTRATION 35. *Overhead Pass, the Pass.*

hands or arms. The defensive man is thus unable to determine exactly when the pass is to be made.

The Chest Pass

When one thinks of passing as a part of basketball, he usually thinks of the chest pass. In early basketball days it was used almost to the exclusion of all other passing methods. It is still a fine technique. The player who cannot execute this pass well is most limited. It was not listed first because many teams and coaches have limited their teaching of passing to the chest pass alone. No one pass is sufficient, and this holds just as true for the chest pass.

The chest pass is good for medium range passing. Both hands on the ball give the pass plenty of power. It is easy to guide and to control. Split vision can be used most effectively while making a chest pass.

Starting Position. The ball should be started from a position close to the chest, thereby giving it its name. Earlier teachers have advocated a stepping toward the receiver, looking directly at the receiver, a follow through, all of which telegraph the pass too much. It is still necessary for beginners to look rather directly at their receivers. However, it is to be desired that the passer do everything possible to keep from telegraphing.

Start with one foot already advanced, instead of stepping.

ILLUSTRATION 36. *Chest Pass, Start.*

The Pass. If the ball is held close, it can be snapped off without any drawback motion. It should be snapped, rather than pushed with the old exaggerated follow-through action. The actual force is still applied by extension of the wrists and inward snap of the thumbs, just as it was done in 1891. There is no need to extend the arms, since that is extra unneeded force and it tends to telegraph and slow the pass up a bit. The beginner, however, might *need* the extra force created by the extension of both arms. Therefore, we suggest that the beginner *look* at the receiver and *extend* both arms.

ILLUSTRATION 37.   *Chest Pass, Beginner.*

It is desirable for the learner to use less arm extension and more split vision as he progresses in basketball ability. Here is an illustration of the chest pass by a highly skilled performer. Note that he merely snaps the ball off with his hands and wrists. He is using a slight amount of peripheral vision.

ILLUSTRATION 38.   *Chest Pass, Advanced.*

One-Hand Baseball Pass

Baseball passing has lost some popularity in recent years. Some teams are eliminating it entirely from their repertoire of passes. They have found that it is difficult to aim and throw in a straight line. It has a tendency to curve during flight and usually has a good deal of spin, causing it to be hard to catch. Yet, it is about the only pass strong enough for use by most fast break teams who consistently use a long half-court pass out. It is about the only one that can be used for a full court pass, if that necessity should ever arise.

The advantages and disadvantages should be pointed out to each player. He should be warned that it is a most difficult pass to make accurately. It should be taught to beginners, since it is a good prelude to the teaching of one-hand push passing.

Starting Position. Passing with one hand from the shoulder has been aptly named baseball passing because of its similarity to throws made by baseball players. The left foot should be advanced at the beginning of the pass. Both hands should be placed on the ball with the right hand (for a righthanded pass) squarely behind the ball. The left arm will be held low enough for the passer to see over it. The fingers of the right hand should be well spread, creating as large a throwing area as possible.

The Pass. As the pass is started, the left hand comes off the ball. The right hand and arm are swung forward in a straight

ILLUSTRATION 39. *Baseball Pass, Start.*

overhand throw. If the throw is made sidearm style, it will probably curve. The right hand should push straight through the ball
to prevent spin or curving. There should be a slight backspin on
the ball if the straight overhand throw is executed properly. The
left foot slides even farther forward with the pass, and the right
shoulder and arm follow through fully. The passer has little
chance to use any split vision, due to the necessity of concentrating on his target. It is assumed that his target is open and
that there is little need for use of split vision.

ILLUSTRATION 40.   *Baseball Pass, Follow Through.*

The Hook Pass

The hook pass is another pass that is being used less and less.
At one time it ranked next to the chest pass in frequency of use.
Players have learned that it takes longer to get it off and that it
is too easily telegraphed. However, there are still several opportunities for use of the hook pass. Forwards driving the baseline
find that they can hook from that spot to the pivot if their drive
is blocked. Some teams use it as an initial pass out from the defensive board to start a fast break. Pivot men use it from a standing position to feed cutters, especially weak side cutters or those
not cutting close to the pivot man. Occasionally, guards find it
appropriate for feeding the post man, especially if he is a tall
player.

Since the hook pass is made with one hand, it is necessary to
develop skill with both right and left hands. This is another reason
why it is good to teach beginners to use the hook pass. They de-

velop as a secondary objective better use of both hands, becoming a little more ambidextrous during the process. They learn to coordinate leg and arm motion on either side. It will have some carryover value toward learning the lay-up from either side of the basket. Learning of the hook pass and lay-up shooting drills might well follow each other in sequence during the practice schedule, to get full benefit from this carryover quality. Taller youngsters, who will later need to learn the hook shot, will find the motion used in passing very similar.

Starting Position. The starting position for beginners should be with the side to the target or the receiver. Assuming the passer is making a throw with his right hand, he can then step out with the left foot and see his receiver clearly. Most beginners will want to step straight away from the target. This only heightens the difficulty of an already difficult pass.

The ball should be held high and slightly to the right side of the chest. The head should be turned toward the receiver. The right hand will be spread and placed squarely behind the ball. Fingers should grip the ball with a moderate amount of tension.

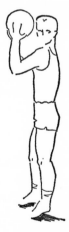

ILLUSTRATION 41. *Hook Pass, Start.*

The Pass. The passer will step out with his left foot, just as he does in shooting a lay-up. After planting his left foot, he lifts his right knee and starts the ball overhead and slightly in front of the face, so that he can see his receiver. As the right arm swings upward, the left arm is removed and pulled to the rear in preparation for a follow through. Every effort should be made to throw the ball in a straight line without any spin other than a small amount of backspin.

ILLUSTRATION 42.

Sideward Hook

This pass is a natural follow-up to the regular hook pass. It is the same motion executed from the side. It is used at times when the passer needs to get the ball by an opponent who has already

ILLUSTRATION 43.　*Sideward Hook.*

given him some angle advantage. It can be used to hit the outside hand of the breaking forward receiving from a guard.

The side hook is executed by taking a step forward with the foot opposite to the passing hand.

Two-Hand Pass

A good safe method of making hand-offs to cutters is essential to pivot men. The two-hand underhand pass is a natural follow-up to the hand-off pass. It is made in the same manner, except that the ball follows a flat trajectory. The two-hand underhand pass is used best by a pivot man passing to wide cutters who are about six or eight feet from him.

The passer will step toward his receiver and start the pass from his waist. The pass is made simply by extending both arms toward the receiver and releasing the ball as the arms reach a full extension.

ILLUSTRATION 44.

Here is a good drill to help in the development of the underhand pass. It also helps to teach players the proper time for its use. It would be well to have the cutters break close to the passer for the hand-offs to start the drill, as in diagram A. As they warm up, have them break wider and take the underhand pass.

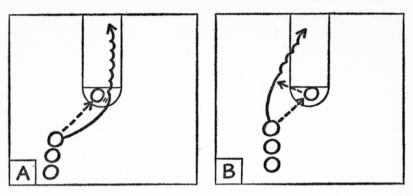

ILLUSTRATION 45.

One-Hand Push Pass

Here is a pass the players themselves have developed. Since they use it constantly, it might as well be taught. It has come about as a natural offshoot of the baseball pass. Actually, it is quite different.

The one-hand push pass should be used for short passing. Guards find it useful in passing to their forwards in a single post system. There are times when forwards can use it to feed post men. It is a little more accurate than baseball passing, which is the most dangerous of styles.

Starting Position. This pass starts out just as if it were going to be a two-hand chest pass. The major difference in the starting position lies in the fact that the one-hand push should be carried slightly toward the side to be used in passing. If the right hand is to be used, the ball is carried to the right side of the chest. It is also well to advance the right foot. The right hand will be placed behind the ball while the left rests on its side, much as the hands are fixed for a one-hand shot.

The Pass. The passer pushes with both arms from shoulder height. When they are about halfway through their extension, the left hand will come off and the right hand will continue its extension, pushing the ball toward the receiver. The right hand is kept behind the ball at all times until it is released.

It is obvious that in carrying the ball to one side, a greater advantage of angle is created if some advantage already exists. It

ILLUSTRATION 46.

would be somewhat better than the chest pass in such an instance. Since the ball is kept at shoulder level and the pass is short, it is more accurate and easier to control than the baseball pass. It is, therefore, the best of each, combined for use in a special situation.

ILLUSTRATION 47.

Here is a drill using the one-hand push from guard to forward. Note that the defensive man is already at a disadvantage. As players become more skilled, they should use split vision to keep the defensive man guessing whether the pass will go to the pivot or to the forward. The drill should be run to both sides of the floor so that the left hand will also be developed.

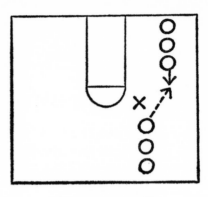

ILLUSTRATION 48.

PASSING SUMMARY

There are no behind-the-back passes offered here. There are no blind passing styles recommended. The Globe Trotters get paid to pass behind their backs. If a player wants to pass from behind his back, he should be encouraged to join the Trotters or some other professional team which specializes in entertainment.

When each player takes pride in completing every pass and learns fully what an incompleted pass means to his team, the problem of teaching passing is half done. An incomplete pass usually means that the passer is *giving* his opponents 1⅓ points. Ball possession is worth 1⅓ points to a good team.

It is doubtful if the team starring one man will have good passing. The coach should examine his offense if there is no sound pass work. Players who are rarely involved in scoring maneuvers are not anxious to become the leaders in assists. If the offense allows balanced ball handling, each player will be less reluctant to pass at proper times.

Passing styles and drills should be closely related to the particular offensive style of the team. It is well to incorporate a part of the offense into passing drills whenever possible. In this way you make sure that each player can execute the passes necessary to make the offense "go."

Praise the good, unselfish feeder. The scorers cannot score unless they get the ball. Many high scorers have been indebted to an unsung hero who consistently and accurately fed him the ball.

TEACHING POINTERS

1. Avoid cross-court passing.
2. Pass to a point somewhere between waist and chest level.
3. Lead moving cutters.
4. Pass at a speed that can be caught, but don't "float" the ball.
5. Use some split vision, but don't pass blindly.
6. Don't pass to receivers who won't move to meet the ball.

RECEIVING

Anytime a basketball is thrown, it must be caught. In past years the throwing has been well emphasized. All coaches strive to build good passing teams. Catching has been neglected. Close observation and records of game errors reveal that the majority of ball losses are caused by poor receiving rather than by poor passing.

Passes are often missed because they are taken for granted. The basketball is large and receivers assume it is easily caught. They would be correct in this assumption if the defensive men would not interfere. They would be correct if they were extremely well poised and did not allow game time nerves to turn every finger into a thumb.

Many passes are missed because receivers simply do not look at the ball until it strikes their hands. They start to dribble or shoot *before* the ball gets into their hands. Unfortunately, the shot or dribble doesn't usually succeed.

Some receivers will not attempt to catch passes that are not thrown perfectly. If the ball is high or wide, they let it go. It is true that the resulting shot or movement will be impeded by a poorly thrown pass, but receivers must be conditioned to go for every pass, no matter how wild it may be. Possession of the ball is worth too much to allow players to develop a casual attitude.

It is obvious that every passing drill also creates opportunity for receiving practice. Receiving will be better taught, however, by treating it separately. This will hold true especially for beginners. As the players progress in skill, passing and receiving practice may well be conducted as one drill.

Good receivers must catch passes thrown from many angles and at varying speeds. For study purposes, we will list and illustrate the four positions of primary importance. These positions are created by the necessity of catching passes thrown perfectly, high, low and to moving receivers. There are some principles that apply to receiving all passes. We will consider these principles as we analyze the action of catching a well-thrown pass.

Basic Principles of Receiving

1. *Watching the Ball.* Good baseball outfielders learn to look intently at a baseball until it actually plunks into the glove. Basketball receivers should imitate this type of visual concentration while catching. Split vision is of no value to a receiver. He should keep his head down for the average pass, so that his eyes can follow the ball right into his hands.

ILLUSTRATION 49.

2. *Concentration.* Practice receiving and game receiving are somewhat different. In practice there is no pressure. It is easy to catch the ball while in the relaxed atmosphere of practice. Players should try to relax during the actual game, but it is doubtful if their muscles can repel the effects of extra adrenalin placed there by the natural function of the body glands. Game time pressures will cause muscles to be a little tighter and will require re-

ceivers to concentrate a little harder. If the habit of concentrating is not developed in practice, it cannot be developed at game time.

3. *Hand and Arm Readiness.* Preparing the hands and arms for catching can be done in a split second but it should be done *before* the ball arrives. It cannot be taken for granted that there is still plenty of time. The receiver will *reach* for the ball as he steps or breaks to meet it. All passes should be met. Sometimes it may consist of only one step or even just a forward lean. Meeting the ball prevents interceptions and discourages further attempts.

The elbows should be slightly bent so that the ball will not be stiff-armed. The arms are extended with the fingers spread, like those of a football end catching a spot pass. The thumbs are closer together than the forefingers. Many coaches teach receiving with one hand *behind* the ball and one to the side. This procedure would surely lessen the number of passes that go through the hands. However, beginners would be confused and would have trouble fixing the ball properly for a subsequent pass. We believe it is best to teach the simple procedure illustrated here, with the coach choosing the procedure he feels to be the best for more advanced performers.

ILLUSTRATION 50.

4. *Catching with the Fingers.* Of course, the thumbs are used in catching but we will consider them as one of the fingers. The main point is not to allow receivers to catch with the palms. It will result in stiff-arming the pass.

ILLUSTRATION 51.

5. *Cushioning Shock of the Ball.* The amount of cushion needed will depend on speed of the ball. Hard passes will require more than soft passes. Receivers should develop the habit of allowing their arms to *give* with the ball after it strikes their fingers. The habit of giving with a pass will help immensely when catching hard passes. It consists of flexing both arms and drawing the ball toward the chest in one motion.

ILLUSTRATION 52.

6. *Catching with Both Hands.* It is amazing how many two-armed players try to handicap themselves by catching with one hand. Only as a last resort should a receiver reach for the ball with one arm and hand. One-armed receiving is ineffectual, prevents a good pass or shot from resulting, and causes the receiver to be easily shaken loose from the ball.

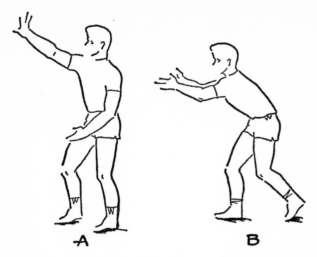

ILLUSTRATION 53. *(A) Wrong. (B) Right.*

7. *Grasping the Ball Firmly.* While relaxation is desired during receipt of the ball, it is desirable to grasp the ball firmly once it is in the receiver's possession. Firm possession discourages defensive players from bumping receivers or "digging" for the ball. A receiver will be better protected if he will bring the ball in close to his lower chest region. Such action results in a slight spread of his elbows which affords him further protection.

8. *Bending the Knees.* There are few skills in basketball that can be performed from a straight-legged position. Receivers are

ILLUSTRATION 54.

in poor position to adjust to high or low passes if the legs are not flexed to an alert stance. Bent legs will allow the receiver to drive or shoot more easily also.

ILLUSTRATION 55.

Receiving Low Passes

Catching the low pass has caused many tall pivot men great frustration. The player wants the ball from waist to chest level, the coach wants the ball thrown at that level, and the passer wants to get the ball to the receiver at that level; nevertheless, as long as players are mortal, there will be some low passes during the course of a season. Guards and forwards will get their share of this type pass, but it is usually the pivot who gets more than any other player.

To catch a low pass, the receiver must alter the position of his hands slightly and bend his knees more. The receiver who normally meets passes with bent knees will not have much trouble

ILLUSTRATION 56.

with low passes. He can bend a little lower and turn his palms up so that the little fingers are together. This action is not unlike that of the baseball catcher who has to receive a low pitch, except that the basketball receiver uses both hands.

Receiving High Passes

It is highly possible that the too-high pass is the most difficult of all to receive. Experiments have proved that the arms can be lowered more quickly than they can be raised. If a receiver meets the ball properly and bends his knees, an unexpected high pass requires that he straighten up and raise his arms quickly. There are limits to one's overhead reach, whereas the floor creates a boundary below which low passes cannot go.

To catch high passes a receiver will turn his thumbs together while his palms open toward the ball. He should reach for the ball when possible, so that there will be some shock cushion for hard passes. There is a possibility that the receiver will even have to jump to catch some high passes. If so, he will merely attempt to secure it for ball possession, for he will probably be too far off balance for a scoring effort. If he has to jump for the ball his hand position will be the same as that shown here for a high pass.

In catching high passes there is a natural tendency for the receiver not to raise his head. If he does not raise his head, however, his eye level will be parallel to the floor and prevent him from seeing the ball. As a consequence, he will not catch most high passes.

ILLUSTRATION 57.

The Cutting Receiver

A moving receiver coming straight toward a pass will catch just as if he were a regular receiver. Almost all receivers will be moving, but a fast-cutting receiver is different.

To hit the cutter from one side, so that he can receive and continue his drive, is necessary in nearly all pattern type offenses. This type cutter will have to bring his arms up in readiness for the pass. He should take the pass slightly in front of his chest. If the pass is to his right side, he will turn the upper trunk somewhat toward the pass, while his hips are kept straight, as he continues his cut, waiting for the ball to arrive. His eyes are focused even more intently on the ball, because he might have to stop or speed up to receive it if it is improperly thrown.

ILLUSTRATION 58.

Some fast break teams will find it necessary to hit cutters moving directly away from the ball. The passer must "lead" such receivers a considerable distance, according to the distance between passer and receiver and according to the speed of the cutter.

This receiver will take the ball over his shoulder with the little fingers turned together and his thumbs outward. He should attempt to get his fingers on the ball so that he can continue his drive by dribbling. This means he must get the ball to the floor quickly.

ILLUSTRATION 59.

Passing and Receiving Drills

Here are two all-time favorite passing drills. These drills allow the teacher to emphasize all aspects of passing. Players will develop split vision, and they will learn proper passing speeds, not to telegraph, to pass *by* defenders and to catch the ball.

1. Two-Ball Drill.   Two basketballs are put into play and kept moving at all times. There are one receiver and five passers. Each man attempts to help the receiver by not passing until he can readily receive.

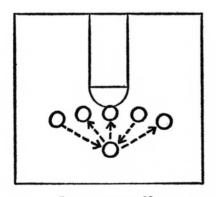

ILLUSTRATION 60.

2. Bull in the Ring. This drill teaches players early that they must get the ball to an open teammate with defenders interfering. When the defensive man in the middle deflects or intercepts a pass, the one who threw the ball will take his place.

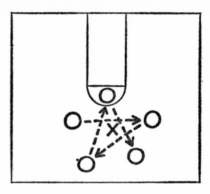

ILLUSTRATION 61.

Receiving Drills

1. Baseline Cut. When forwards are overplayed, they must be able to break down the baseline, catch the ball and lay it up.

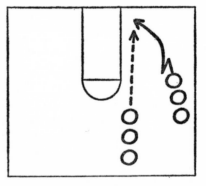

ILLUSTRATION 62.

2. Bad Pass Drill. Pair the players off in twos. Have them purposely pass high, low or wide to each other. This drill will teach receivers to be alert for movements in any direction.

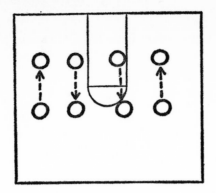

ILLUSTRATION 63.

5. Dribbling

Dribbling has been abused so often that many coaches have developed a negative attitude toward this fine skill. Lecturers at coaching clinics usually wind up by saying, "Don't dribble at all if possible." Dr. Naismith, who invented the sport of basketball, frowned on too much use of the dribble. At one time dribbling was almost ruled illegal by the rules makers. Most of us teach our players dribbling with reservations. At the same time that we are teaching it, we fear that it will be used improperly.

The dribble has an important place in the game of basketball. If it were eliminated entirely, this fact would be in visible evidence. It should be taught positively and without any reservations. Every member of the squad should develop dribble skill. The forwards and centers in an average game appear ludicrous if they have to dribble; the primary reason for this is that they have been excluded from dribble drills. There is no need to fear overuse of this skill any more than there is a need to fear overuse of shooting or passing. You need to caution the players concerning overuse or wrong use of shooting; yet a positive approach is usually taken to the teaching of shooting. Caution players on the wrong use of dribbling, but teach it to all players in a positive manner.

It is improbable that all the occasions for dribbling can be listed. Here are some of the more common occasions when skilled dribbling may be needed.

1. To advance the ball to front court.
2. To drive through defensive gaps for scoring.

3. To carry the ball down the middle on a fast break.
4. To escape pressing defensive tactics.
5. To clear a congested area under the goal after a defensive rebound.
6. To get out of trouble if no teammate is available for receiving.

There are four major types of dribble used in the course of an average ball game. These types must necessarily be taught to each player. They are the basic dribble form, low dribble, change of pace dribble, and change of direction dribble.

BASIC DRIBBLE FORM

This form is advocated in lieu of a so-called high dribble. No occasions arise during the course of a game for the use of a high dribble. Even in advancing the ball to the front court, basic dribbling form should be used.

It is necessary to drill players in using right and left hands when teaching dribbling. A dribbler who can go only one way is too easily stymied. In all discussions of technique and drill we will assume that an equal amount of time will be spent on development of each hand.

1. Foot movements at beginning and end of a dribble

For a dribble to be legal, the ball must leave the dribbler's hand before his rear foot leaves the floor. This rule is often violated. Sometimes it is penalized and sometimes it is not. Players become confused and actually afraid of their footwork. Since doubt and confusion only cause them to make more errors, the best policy is to teach your players the proper method of initiating the dribble. They should not be allowed to violate this procedure even though they see other teams get away with violations. Nationally televised games in which players violate this rule have caused a great deal of confusion in the minds of young players. If they learn the right way, they will be prepared on those nights when strong officiating penalizes such mistakes.

Terminating a dribble properly is more difficult than starting one. Momentum of drive and body causes young players to take one step too many. To learn how to stop properly, the dribble

ILLUSTRATION 64.

should be performed first at slow speeds that can be controlled. Dribblers should never try to exceed a controlled speed limit, no matter how skilled they become. A two-footed halt with bent legs offers a performer best opportunity for subsequent movement. He can then establish *either* foot as the pivotal base. To be legal, the dribbler must not take more than one step after catching the ball to end his dribble.

ILLUSTRATION 65.

2. Head and eyes

A common error of beginners is keeping the head down so low that open teammates cannot be spotted. Yet, it is not necessary to pull the head up so high that the ball is completely unrelated to anything but the dribbler's hand. If the head is held comfortably up, the dribbler can spot open teammates and maintain *visual* contact with the ball by use of marginal vision.

Many of us have overemphasized keeping the head up. While some young players think it is wrong if the eye should spot the ball momentarily, the greatest professional players will admit that they maintain visual contact with the ball. We are not advocating that the dribbler look at the ball, or even that he duck his head occasionally, which many players do. We simply say that there is no harm done and that better control is maintained if the dribbler keeps slight visual *contact*.

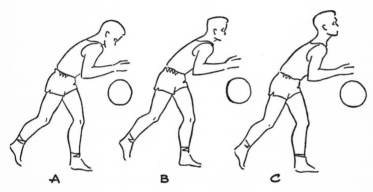

ILLUSTRATION 66.   *(A) Wrong   (B) Right   (C) Unnecessary.*

You cannot overemphasize the bad effects of keeping the head so low that open receivers are not spotted. The dribbler should constantly survey the changing pattern of teammates and opponents before him, so that he knows where all these men are at each moment. Dribble "blinders" are now on the market at economical prices. These glasses prevent the dribbler from seeing the ball unless it is bounced very high. Such practices will help to teach him to look out beyond for other players.

The following is a dribble relay that will also help. Notice that dribblers start at either end of a row of chairs. They must ultimately pass each other at some point during the dribble. If they do not look up and ahead they will collide with each other. Such a possibility virtually insures development of the correct technique.

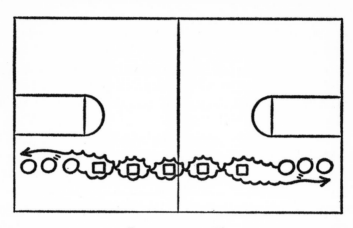

ILLUSTRATION 67.

3. Body and leg position

The body leans forward into the dribble. It should not be overbalanced. Most of the lean occurs from the waist up. Weight should be balanced primarily on the balls of the feet. Legs should be bent more than is normal in average walking. The shoulder opposite the dribbling hand should be slightly forward.

ILLUSTRATION 68.

4. Arm, wrist and hand action

The upper arm should be advanced so that the elbow is several inches in front of the waist. The lower arm is extended forward on a line parallel to the floor. Wrist action is performed from a semi-locked position. The fingers are spread and the hand is cupped to conform to ball shape. Action of the forearm, wrist and hand is best described as a *pushing* or *pumping* motion. The hand pushes down past the parallel three or four inches and remains there until the ball comes back up to meet it. When the ball rebounds into the cupped hand, ball and hand "ride" up past a line parallel to the floor about three or four inches. The hand then pushes down again in the same action, which is repeated over and over.

The main point is that the ball and hand are touching for a brief period of time as the arm comes up for the pump. There is

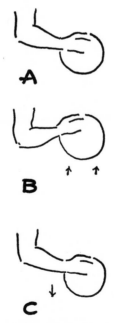

ILLUSTRATION 69. (A) *Ball Makes Contact.* (B) *Ball Rides Up.* (C) *Pump for Next Dribble.*

no slapping motion. While ball and hand touch, the dribbler can adjust speeds, direction or distance of ball from the body, *etc.* The pumping action is moderate in strength. There is no need to pound the ball or test the air in it. Pounding dribbles are hard to control.

5. Speed of dribbler

Dribbling errors are created in great part by overestimating one's "controlled" dribble speed. It is foolish to move at a rate of speed that cannot be controlled. Usually the "control" speed for high school and college-age boys will be about three-fourths of their regular speed. Obviously, beginners in grade or junior high will need to move even slower. A good rule of thumb for a player of any age or skill category is to *dribble at that rate of speed that allows him to control his body and the ball.* He must be ready to cut if a defensive man steps in front of him. He should be able to stop quickly for a jump shot if the opportunity presents itself. He cannot execute a good change of pace motion if he is already dribbling at top speed.

6. Height of dribble

If the dribbler's hand should purposely miss the ball on his pumping action, the ball should rise to about *chest height* for that individual. If it is suspected that a boy is pounding too hard, have him try this little experiment. Pounders who give the ball a

ILLUSTRATION 70.

beating every time they dribble are aptly labeled "air testers." At the other extreme, some boys seem to be afraid that they will damage the ball and do not give it enough impetus.

7. Distance of dribble from body

If the dribbler has taken the proper body lean, he will have no difficulty in keeping the ball away from his feet. A straight-up position will cause him to overrun the ball. Distance of the ball out front will depend upon his rate of speed. Moving at moderate speed, the ball will strike the floor slightly to the right of his right foot (right hand), and six inches in front, if ball and foot arrive at the same time. Moving at greater speed, the ball will be pushed farther from the body and more in front of the right foot.

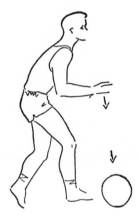

ILLUSTRATION 71.

8. Use of free arm

The free arm affords some protection of the ball if used properly and legally. It can legally be raised and flexed, but any elbowing action would be penalized. If the dribbler accustoms himself to keeping his free arm slightly up and flexed, he will find it a useful psychological, if not physical, barrier to the defensive man. It is more important to maintain this position when driving by an opponent than any other time.

ILLUSTRATION 72.

Low Dribble

A low dribble action will be executed in fundamentally the same way, utilizing good basic form. Height of the dribble, distance from the body and speed will vary some. The body should be crouched, resulting in a lower bounce of the ball. Defensive players will have less chance to steal the ball from a low dribbler. The ball is kept closer to the body and more to the right of his leg. Speed will be reduced for greater maneuverability in congested areas. The free arm is brought higher for better ball protection. A little more turning of the shoulder will also create better protection for the ball.

Change of Pace

Changing pace and rhythm often helps keep the defense guessing and allows the dribbler to move unrestrictedly. Diving for the ball when a dribbler is constantly varying speeds is too hazardous. Defensive players will commit fouls unnecessarily. The change of pace is also a good scoring maneuver. It will often fool the defensive man completely and allow the dribbler to go in for a lay-up. When a young player has learned to dribble safely, encourage him to practice dribbling and skipping simultaneously. It gives him rhythm and confidence. Skipping action is good for change of pace motion, too. It should not be tried until the dribbler has developed good basic form.

The change of pace is executed best at about half speed. If the dribbler is using his right hand, he will stop with his left foot forward, hesitate briefly and move off again at a faster rate of speed. If his left foot is forward, he can maintain proper body lean as he starts off after the hesitation. Later, it will allow him to change speeds and directions at the same time. A straightening of the body adds to the illusion that he is really stopping completely and draws defensive men close enough to drive around. When he steps out after pausing, that stride should be quite long.

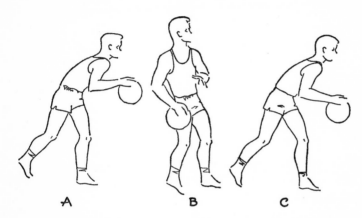

ILLUSTRATION 73. (A) Stop. (B) Pause. (C) Go.

Change of Direction

Changing directions successfully is essential to good dribbling. Guards advancing the ball to front court will be continually harassed if they always move in a straight line. Pressing teams enjoy catching a dribbler who cannot successfully deviate from a straight path. Basket drivers must be able to change directions quickly to prevent numerous charging fouls.

A dribbler performing with his right hand will cut left after planting his right foot. To turn right, he will cut after planting his left foot. Caution players against "palming" or carrying the ball. The hand must be placed on the top right or top left of the ball according to the change in direction. It *must not* be placed *underneath* the ball. If the hand is placed underneath, a rolling of the wrist will result which, if legal, would give dribblers a great advantage.

A change of speed is almost necessary to execute a good change of direction. Otherwise, the dribbler will be unable legally to drive the ball in a new direction while maneuvering his body at the same time. Young players should be encouraged to slow up when changing directions. As they progress in skill, the turn can be made at faster speeds.

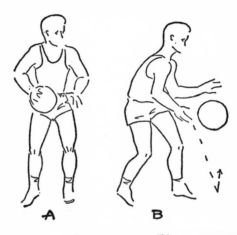

ILLUSTRATION 74.

There are many occasions for use of the dribble other than the major situations listed here. Fake and drive, receiving and dribbling as a cutter, pivot and dribble, dribble and pass are some of the occasions involving a dribble. Let us take a closer look at the fake and drive.

The fake may consist of a false shooting motion to draw the defensive man up, a feint with the feet, a fake passing motion or a simple movement of the head. The objective is to draw the defensive man to you or to draw him to one side or the other.

Here is a fake left and drive right. A long left stride is taken to lure the defensive man slightly left. The right foot is already established as the pivot foot; so the first actual dribbling step is taken with a cross-over of the left foot. Also, the fake and drive may be with the same foot.

ILLUSTRATION 75. (A1,2) *Fake Left, Drive Right.*
(B1,2,3) *Fake Right, Drive Right.*

Here is a good forward-to-forward pass that the entire squad
can perform. Guards and pivot men need this sort of skill just as
much as the forwards. It helps cutters learn to receive on the
move, drop the ball to the floor and continue their drive by use
of the dribble without any undue loss of time. Many mistakes in
footwork are made by so-called advanced performers because
they were not drilled properly on this maneuver early in their
careers. The rule book says that the ball must leave the hands
during the course of one and one-half strides.

The above drill can be altered slightly to include yet another
necessary dribble situation. The receiver will catch the ball, stop
successfully, pivot and dribble for a lay-up with the outside hand.

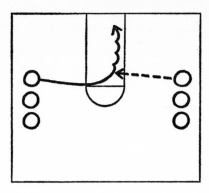

ILLUSTRATION 76A.

Be sure to run these drills right *and* left. The angle can be altered to give pivot men an almost true game situation drill, as in diagram 2.

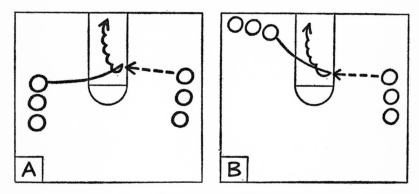

ILLUSTRATION 76B.

TEACHING HINTS

1. Teach the legal aspects of starting and stopping of the dribble first.
2. Watch for palming on change of pace and change of direction moves.
3. Double dribble—striking the ball with both hands—is a common beginner's error that must be watched for.
4. Never allow a player to *waste* a dribble. Beginners like to bounce it once before passing or shooting. It is a good idea

to make them forfeit possession of the ball any time they waste the dribble in this manner.

5. Don't allow "air testing."
6. Teach dribblers to move at a controlled speed.
7. Don't allow head-down dribbling.
8. Teach beginners to protect the ball. Always keep the ball on the side opposite to the defensive man.
9. Penalize dribblers in some manner if they use the dribble when a pass would have been better.
10. Be sure to include big men in dribble drills.

6. Rebounding and Tipping

Good rebounders *can* be developed. There is much that can be done to help a boy develop physically, but the first step is to "sell" him on the importance of rebounding. The good rebounder should experience a sense of achievement as great as that of the prolific scorer. The greatest admiration and praise should be his.

Building the Proper Attitude Toward Rebounding

Various psychological approaches can be used which will help instill the right attitude in the entire team. The statistical sheet is a device many coaches use. Call out the number of offensive and defensive rebounds at the half of each game. Post charts with these figures on them on the bulletin board so that the student body can read them. Each player will strive to be the high rebounder. This rivalry can be an open one, whereas most coaches frown on such open competition between scorers. The statistical sheet forces boys who want only to score to become better rounded in order to maintain the respect of their teammates.

An award given to the best rebounder of the season also serves to emphasize this fundamental. The players will keep close check on the statistical charts and some real battles should result. The team should know that this award is to be given. An announcement should be made concerning the award when practice first starts.

Courage is an important factor in rebounding. The team should be reminded of this often. Modern youngsters are always looking for a way of demonstrating their courage. One of the main appeals that athletics has for the teenager is the opportunity it provides for him to prove himself to his friends, to his parents, and, in many cases, to himself. Basketball was once considered a noncontact sport. However, the rules have been modified to overlook contact which is incidental or in which two players are striving for the ball. The coach needs to refer to the fact that rebounding ability is a good test of courage. Courage plus leg strength, plus hard work, make the outstanding rebounder.

Praise is an excellent way to get extra effort. Offer loud vocal praise to the lad who consistently gets under the goal and "mixes" for the rebound. If this lad is a bit shorter than other players who are not doing as well, the praise will serve a double purpose. It will inspire the boy who is praised and will cause the others to double their efforts.

Watching films of professional or good college rebounders is an inspiration to beginners. They see this important skill demonstrated properly by performers who are acutely aware of its value.

"Needling" should be used sparingly if at all by most coaches. Some coaches can use a gentle "needle" very effectively. These coaches know and understand each player as an individual. It is a delicate matter, to be used with caution and then only as a last resort. It can be done by praising a small opponent who is cleaning the boards very courageously. This implies a doubt of the courage of one's own players without actually saying it. Compare a small guard who is an excellent rebounder with a taller boy on the team who is not doing as well. This will needle the taller lad. It is a slightly more subtle way of challenging the boy—of saying, "I dare you to be a man."

Make the first explanation, demonstration and practice of the rebound as memorable an experience as possible. To do so, bring as many of the techniques mentioned into play as possible. If the player's introduction to rebounding is a strong one and constant attention is given this phase of the game as he matures, he will realize the importance of this skill and develop an ideal attitude.

Developing the Ability to Jump Vertically

Some boys can jump well on the first try—others cannot. At first glance the coach might assume that this is a natural phenomenon. Closer examination will almost always reveal that the best jumpers have had previous jumping experience. Even so, there is some difference in potential of individuals. However, every normal boy can learn to jump adequately for the game of basketball.

The first step is to measure the jumping ability of each player. This is easily done by the Sargent test. To use the Sargent test, place a performer beside a wall with a piece of chalk. Have him stand straight and reach upward to make a chalk mark on the wall as high as he can reach without holding the chalk by his fingertips or standing on tiptoe (Ill. A). After taking the starting position, the performer squats and jumps as high as he can. At the peak of his jump he makes another mark. The distance between the two marks is measured to get the actual height of his jump. (Ill. B).

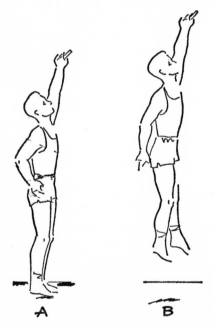

ILLUSTRATION 77. (A) Starting Position. (B) Jump.

A good jump for a beginner in the eighth grade is about 20 inches. Some great jumpers with experience will go above 30 inches. A boy with large legs and small feet or large feet and small legs may suffer some handicap. Boys with long arms which add to their reach have an advantage in actual rebounding, but this doesn't help them on the test.

After measuring the individual's vertical jumping ability, the next step is to improve the ability of each from that shown by the test. To accomplish this phase of the jumper's development, additional strength and/or better jumping techniques must be gained. Strength can be acquired by the proper use of weights. The full squat, hack lift and toe raise are excellent weight conditioners for the large muscles of the legs.

ILLUSTRATION 78. *(A) Full Squat. (B) Hack Lift. (C) Toe Raise.*

The knees can be strengthened by various apparatuses usually found in training rooms. The leg extending exercise from a supine position is an excellent method of strengthening the knees.

ILLUSTRATION 79.

Calisthenics may be used for gaining the strength needed for good jumping. The full squat is a good one. The squat jumper is also good. It is performed by leaping up from a squatting position and returning to the same position. This places great strain on the legs, thereby causing muscle development. Use a volleyball for consecutive jumping and tapping against a wall. Challenge each older performer to tap the ball successfully fifty times before stopping. The high school senior should be able to do fifty jumps if he is in good condition. Beginners will have to build up gradually to this number.

ILLUSTRATION 80.   (A) Full Squat.   (B) Squat Jumper.

After developing strength, new jumping techniques should be introduced. The first job here is to get the boy to *bend* his legs.

ILLUSTRATION 81. *Wall Tapping.*

It seems amazing that many boys will try to jump without bending the knees.

An exercise made famous by the Army physical fitness program is a good way to begin. This exercise is called the high jumper. It is performed in four counts. The performer takes up a position with knees bent, head up and trunk bent forward. The arms are swung to the rear in the starting position. At the count of one, the performer swings his arms forward by executing a low jump or vertical hop. At the count of two, he swings his arms back to the rear by executing another low hop. At the count of three, he jumps vertically off the ground as high as possible, using a strong upswing of the arms and stretching the arms overhead. At the count of four the performer returns to the starting position by executing another low hop after striking the floor at the conclusion of count three. By doing the slight jump at the end of count three, he can return to the starting position more smoothly in preparation for the next sequence.

A fairly recent exercise, developed by Iowa's Coach Bucky O'Conner, will improve jumping techniques. It is called the bench exercise. Secure a bench to the floor. It should be about the size

ILLUSTRATION 82.

of a regular dressing room bench. Have the performer stand
with his side to the bench and about six inches from it. He should
assume a good jumping position with arms and knees bent. He
jumps sideward and over the bench. As soon as he strikes the
floor on the other side of the bench, he immediately jumps back
over the bench. The number of jumps will be determined by the

degree of strength, experience, and stamina of the performer.
The outstanding jumper can perform about 35 jumps during a
30-second interval.

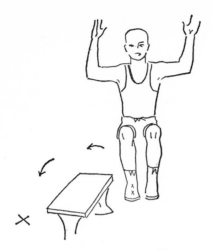

ILLUSTRATION 83.

Another good idea for impressing the players with the necessity
of bending the knees is a standing broad jump contest. Each
contestant squats low and swings his arms vigorously. This should
be a natural movement, almost necessary. Point out to the players
the necessity for assuming the same stance when jumping vertically.

Encourage basketball players to participate in volley ball at
every opportunity during the off season. It gives them practice
in using their newly found jumping ability and improves timing.
Certain track and field events are good transfer skills, for example, the high jump and the pole vault.

Some device should be used to keep the jumping improving
daily after the players become proficient. One way is to set a
pair of pole vault standards up each day and put a crossbar at
a low height. Let each boy jump and touch it. Gradually raise
the bar until the last performer is eliminated. Tapping bars
suspended from the ceiling at various heights also helps. These
and other helpful drills can be found described in greater detail

in my earlier book, *Encyclopedia of Basketball Drills* (Englewood Cliffs, N.J., 1958).

Defensive Rebounding

The defensive player has an advantage in having the inside or ideal position for jumping, but he must not take this advantage for granted. To insure the advantage, drill each beginner on boxing out the offensive player. It is easier to box out the offensive player when he is the shooter. Whether the offensive man is the shooter or not, the defensive man should see the shot. He should watch the offensive man long enough to determine which route the offensive player will take to the goal. He should then pivot in front of the offensive man and move in with his legs wide apart, taking shuffling steps. He should not watch the offensive man too long, for it will throw his timing off on the subsequent jump.

ILLUSTRATION 84.

Getting Rebound Position

Good position for rebounding has been emphasized a great deal in teaching fundamental rebounding. Good position varies with each rebound attempt. Several factors have to be judged almost unconsciously, and reaction must take place immediately. The distance from the goal, trajectory of the ball, and speed of the ball are all factors that involve the position taken by the re-bounder, whether he is on offense or defense. Good position might be considered that which results in possession of the ball. Some boys can leap so high that they can rebound over the back of an opponent without committing a foul. We will discuss here the *ideal* position and the steps for teaching the technique of getting position to beginners.

The first and probably the most important job is to teach the importance of the *inside position* and the methods for gaining this position. The inside position is between the opponent and the goal. Once this position is attained, the rebound should be easily secured if the follow-up efforts are reasonably good. Here is one method of teaching boys how to get the inside position.

Place two players near the goal, with one having the advantage or being nearer to the basket. Toss the ball against the back-board. The nearer boy should get the inside and make every effort to keep the other boy on the outside. To do this, he adjusts constantly, shuffling sideward without crossing his legs. He raises his arms and spreads them firmly, with his elbows projecting rigidly.

To stress the importance of keeping position once it is gained, have the performer maintain position until the ball comes down and strikes the floor. To accomplish this, the inside boy must work hard, keeping his opponent back of himself. He has to be aggressive. His distance from the goal will vary. He must keep a taller boy farther from the goal than a boy his own height. Some boys get too far under the goal; some get too far away. If he gets too far under, his opponent can nudge him on under the basket and rebound over his back. If he gets too far away, his opponent can run around and take the inside at the last second. The best policy is to teach the inside boy to stay inside, rather close, then to step back, nudging the opponent gently away from the goal. To protect that position once it is gained, he should spread his arms and legs, bend his knees and, while keep-ing physical contact with the opponent, stay between him and the basket.

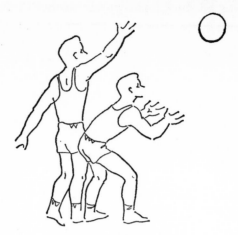

ILLUSTRATION 85.

The Jump

The jump is made *after* the performer has decided where the ball will come off the boards. The majority of boys jump too early or too late. To learn where and when the ball will rebound, a beginner must watch the ball closely. He can improve his timing

ILLUSTRATION 86.

by mentally timing all shots taken by his partner during shooting drills. Good position will cover up for a slight lack of timing. Ideally, the rebounder should get the ball at the peak of his jump. He should utilize the arms by thrusting them vigorously upward, since they should be stretched when he gets the ball. His eyes should be concentrating on the target, which is the ball. The performer should *jump into* the ball rather than leap straight up. This is another procedure for keeping opponents the maximum distance from the ball.

Receiving the Ball

The player should grasp the ball firmly so that, if there is contact, he will not be jarred loose at this crucial point. He should lift the buttocks just enough to keep his opponent from rebounding over his shoulder. Use strong language in describing the way he should receive the ball; words such as clutch, snatch and grab are very expressive. This helps impress upon the rebounder the importance of not losing the ball once it is touched. There are rebound machines on the market which will jerk the ball out of the rebounder's hands if he doesn't hold onto it firmly. Another method of causing this aspect of rebounding to become automatic is to have one boy rebound and another one jar the rebounder just as he touches the ball.

ILLUSTRATION 87.

The Jackknife

In order to insure continued possession of the ball, the rebounder must twist strongly away from his nearest opponent. If the rebounder is on one side of the goal, he will nearly always twist and face the corner of the floor while still in the air. He stays in a pike position to protect the ball. He should draw the ball back slightly toward his hip which is nearest the base line just before landing.

ILLUSTRATION 88.

Landing Position

The rebounder will land facing a corner if his rebound comes from one side of the goal. If the ball comes directly off the front, he simply twists away from the pressure. He lands in a crouch with the feet well spread. The ball is protected by extended elbows. From this position, the performer can pass out or dribble down the base line several steps toward a corner to expedite the pass out. This is also a good position from which to score with the outside hand by jumping back up to bank the ball into the basket.

ILLUSTRATION 89.

Offensive Rebounding

Offensive rebounding is more difficult than defensive rebounding. The defensive player, by the nature of his position, has the inside track. This means that the offensive player must make a special effort to get around and inside the defensive man.

Shooting drills performed in pairs are a good way to practice such maneuvers. The shooter follows through with his shot and then fakes one way before trying to run around his partner for the good position. He may double fake if he is very fast. Remember that the defensive boy cannot tarry too long or his timing on the jump will be poor.

The teacher must assume that offensive rebounding can be just as successful as defensive rebounding. However, where equal stress is placed on both and equal effort is given by the player,

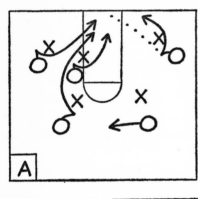
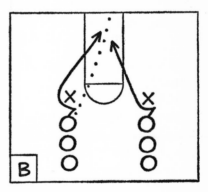
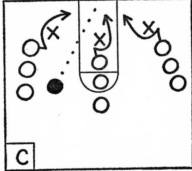

ILLUSTRATION 90.

the charts are going to show more defensive rebounds. Each player needs practice in gaining the inside from his normal offensive spot. Forwards, pivot men and guards will all run these drills from their regular positions. The drills should be designed to practice getting around the defensive man after taking a shot and getting around the defensive man after a teammate has taken a shot.

The pivot men and forwards can be worked together in one drill. The guards can be worked separately. Remember that one offensive man should be a safety, just in case the defensive team gets the ball and attempts a fast break. Three drills are shown below which cover each situation. Note in the team drill that one guard is checking while all other offensive men are moving for the rebound after the right forward's shot.

Tipping

If the offensive player gains the inside position and is well balanced on his jump, he should try to tip the ball back into the

ILLUSTRATION 91. *(A) Grasping the Ball. (B) Tipping It In.*

goal. If he is not on balance, he should grasp the ball and retain possession in the manner described in defensive rebounding.

In making the tap, the beginner should use *both* hands. He should stretch his arms as much as possible, but at the moment of contact he should allow his elbows to bend slightly, so that he will not end up *batting* the ball. The figure below shows the position for a beginner. Beginners should bank the ball off the boards when it is possible.

More advanced performers should be able to tip with either hand. There is much disagreement among coaches concerning the proper method of tipping with one hand. Some think the arms should be completely locked from shoulder to hand at the moment of contact. Others like the elbow and wrist slightly flexed. Some like their tippers to stiffen the fingers and keep them close together. Others like the fingers spread.

We recommend that the elbow and wrist be slightly flexed, the fingers and thumb spread so that the hand is made as wide as possible. The tipper should tip with the fingers and the callous ridge at the base of the fingers—not with fingers alone, and not with the palm. When contact is made, the tipper imparts a soft push to the ball by straightening the arm, wrist and fingers

ILLUSTRATION 92.

completely. The advanced player may tip directly over the rim
or bank the ball.

Every movement of the tipper and the rebounder is the same
until contact is made with the ball. The tipper should *not* try to
raise the buttocks at the time of contact. It is not necessary and
may lessen the over-all height of his jump. By stretching *one*
hand and shoulder he can reach higher than an opponent of his
own height who is attempting to rebound with *both* hands. This
is the one slight advantage the offensive rebounder enjoys; he
should try to use it fully.

Drills to help with the development of tippers can be found in
the *Encyclopedia of Basketball Drills.*

Rebounding the Free Throw

Here is a special rebound situation which is different from the
regular offensive or defensive situations. We will consider here
the movements of the first two rebounders on each side of the
free throw lane.

Naturally, the inside or defensive man has the best position.
To assure the fullest benefit of this advantage, he must take
certain precautions. He should watch the ball intently during
its flight, so that he can determine the precise moment that it
touches the goal. During its flight he should raise his arms, spread
his elbows and lean slightly toward the center of the free throw
line. This leaning is calculated to nudge the offensive rebounder
out of position. When ball and goal touch, he slides into the
lane with his outside foot, leaving the inside foot in its original
position. This requires him to perform a one-eighth pivot forward
on his inside foot. From this point, he makes his jump just as
if he were a defensive rebounder.

The second man on the lane, the offensive rebounder, may
combat his disadvantage by leaning slightly into the pressure
forced against him by the defensive man. He may fake with head
and arms to the middle lane and step around the inside man to
the base line. He should strive to tap the ball back into the
basket or back to the shooter, since he can reach higher with
one hand than his opponent can reach with two hands. If he can
tap the ball back onto the boards, even if he must do this from

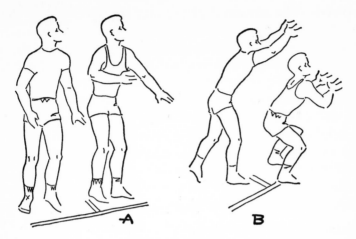

ILLUSTRATION 93.

an off-balance position, he or a teammate might be in better position when it comes off the boards a second time. He is at such a disadvantage initially that this is his best solution to the problem. However, if the offensive rebounder can catch the ball securely enough to come down with it, this is better than an off-balance tap against the board.

TEACHING HINTS

1. "Sell" the boys on rebounding.
2. Develop or improve leg strength after measuring natural ability.
3. Improve jumping techniques.
4. Drill on getting rebound position.
5. Drill on jumping.
6. Drill on grasping the ball firmly.
7. Drill on the jackknife.
8. Drill on the landing position.
9. Drill on rebounding techniques at the free throw lane.
10. Drill on getting offensive rebound position.
11. Drill on two-hand tipping.
12. Drill advanced players on one-hand tipping.

7. Pivoting

Early day basketball coaches included pivot practice in every daily practice plan. Gradually we have drifted away from daily practice of pivoting. Pivoting is practiced while performing fakes, screens, rolls and other drills, and it is assumed that this is sufficient pivot practice. However, there are so many occasions in basketball when a pivot is helpful that it should be taught as a separate skill, just as we teach any other fundamental. Moreover, it is a weapon that can be used by every team member. Pivot men or centers are not the only squad members who need to develop the skill. Nor is it a skill that is limited to use by the player in possession of the ball. A good pivot turn will be useful also to the player who does not have ball possession.

Pivot practice brings some secondary rewards which are not immediately visible. It causes players to gain the better body balance required to perform any skill well. They learn to stay low with the legs bent. It helps in development of stops and starts, with or without the ball. Good pivot practice will cut down the number of footwork errors, such as a pivot foot drag, that normally cause loss of the ball.

Offensive Pivoting

1. *Pivot and drive for goal.* This is the most traditional pivot play. It is the one we usually think about when we consider the word "Pivot." Centers need to develop this move before they can even be considered for the center spot; forwards and guards will have occasions for use of the pivot and drive. We usually think of it as a *reverse pivot* when it is performed by forwards or

guards. Body weight is shifted from the right to the left foot, and the pushoff is made by the right foot. Legs are well bent, with the hips low. The first stride should be long, to cut off the defensive player. The turn can be made either way. It can be made by executing turns of 45, 90, 180 or 270 degrees.

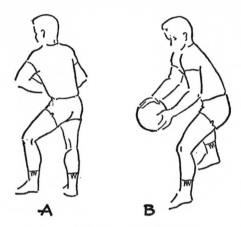

ILLUSTRATION 94.

2. *Ball protection pivot.* The ball should be protected on every move, but the pivot can sometimes be used for that express purpose. When a dribbler is halted by a pressure defensive player and is double teamed, he can elude both men with repeated pivot turns while he gets rid of the ball. If he moves well, he may cause the defensive men to foul him. A halted goal drive leaves the ball unprotected unless a pivot is used immediately. A pivot can be used to protect the ball in front court areas when no receivers are immediately available. The protective pivot is always made to get the body between the ball and the defensive man as quickly as possible. If the defensive man moves, keep the same pivotal base and keep turning to get the body between him and the ball. These movements should be performed while keeping the head up to spot receivers. If a dribble has not already been used, it may get players out of such predicaments.

3. *Roll-off screening pivots.* Nearly all screens terminate with a pivot and roll-out cut. Good screens are set from a balanced

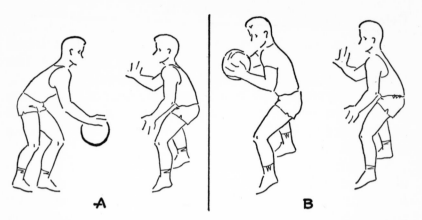

ILLUSTRATION 95.   *Dribble Up to Defensive Man and Pivot.*

position with feet parallel and legs bent. This is also the best stance for pivoting. A good pivot turn gets the defensive man behind the cutter if defensive men are switching.

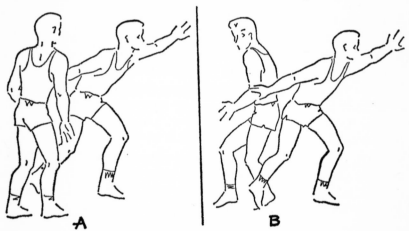

ILLUSTRATION 96.

4. *Pivoting to elude a defensive man.*   The pivot is not always limited to use by players with ball possession. Free lance players can often spring themselves free from defensive men by breaking, stopping and making a quick pivot. They are thus able to place the body in front of the defensive man.

Defensive Pivoting

1. *Cutting out shooters.* A pivot turn is the best known maneuver to keep shooters away from the goal after a shot. This maneuver is explained and illustrated in Chapter Six.

2. *Getting rebound position.* Again, the pivot is used to keep offensive players away from the goal. Such pivots, however, will be performed to cut off players who are not shooting. This move is also explained and illustrated in Chapter Six.

3. *Pivoting during the defensive switch.* Switching defensive players will sometimes be caught by a screen and roll-out. If that happens, the player responsible for the cutter should pivot quickly and break, with the cutter holding his hands high to prevent receipt of a pass.

TEACHING HINTS

1. Place the entire squad on the floor and have them execute pivots of various types upon command.
2. Be sure that each man is low and on balance.
3. Teach defensive pivoting along with offensive pivots.
4. Teach uses of the pivot for players who do not have ball possession.
5. Remember that pivot practice gains the secondary objectives of body balance and alertness.

8. Building an Offensive Team Unit

Before any worthwhile offense can be developed, fundamentals must be well learned. A basketball team attempting to run any offense without sound fundamentals is much like a gardener who has no tools. You surely would be unsuccessful in your efforts if you tried to build a team without the basic tools—fundamentals.

After your players are well on the way to good performance of the fundamentals, it must be decided what type offense to run. Choices are not numerous, but you need to spend a great deal of time making a decision. Basically, there are only three types—a free lance system, set plays or a pattern.

If you run a free lance system, you have probably picked the hardest assignment of your life. Actually, there is no such thing as a free lance basketball team. Players left to their own devices will form certain habits of movement that will occur over and over. They will run certain routes and individual movements habitually. The most difficult task for the coach in operating a free lance system is to keep the players spread. They will have a tendency to bunch up. Unsupervised, a free lance team may sometimes have as many as three pivot men at one time. The other two men might be lined up at right forward. Such alignment does not give you team balance or protection against a fast break if your team loses the ball. Free lance players tend to congregate on the right side of the floor and sometimes all of them will wind up in the right corner if you do not make constant corrections. Of course, many fine teams have operated under the free lance system. It depends on sound fundamentals and close coaching supervision. It is possibly the toughest system of all to run successfully.

Another system is the set play method. Set plays have been run by many championship ball clubs. It is not quite as difficult to run set plays as it is to run a successful free lance system. The great disadvantage is that set plays lack continuity of movement and unusual defenses may demoralize your team at a crucial time. Set plays tend to make a team mechanical in movement. If the play is stymied, players are confused and disconcerted.

The last offensive system you may choose is the pattern system. It is the easiest system of the three, from a teaching standpoint. Of course, you may add the fast break to any one of these systems as a first option, with free lance, set plays or pattern to follow if the fast break does not materialize. Let's assume you have chosen to run a pattern. There are numerous patterns from which to select. An outstanding tall boy or the lack of such a player will have a bearing on the decision. Speed, height and experience of each player will help determine the choice. Young teams, such as eighth grade or "B" teams, will want to choose one that has good continuity and is easy to learn. High school or college teams will want a pattern with more options or greater versatility. If you have average height, with no one extremely large boy, the Drake Shuffle may well be the pattern you are looking for. It is designed to go against a man-to-man defense. We are going to offer here a progressive method of teaching the Drake Shuffle. Remember that it is only one pattern. There are many others to choose from. However, the progression steps for teaching purposes would be much the same, no matter what type pattern is chosen.

A SAMPLE PATTERN

Developing the Drake Shuffle as an Offensive Unit

Bruce Drake developed this pattern, which bears his name. It has become very popular recently in certain areas of the country. As in football, new offensive patterns come and go. Newness and surprise add to their strength. After a team learns the basic movements of the Shuffle, it can be made more versatile by adding variations.

Coach Joel Eaves of Alabama Polytechnic Institute at Auburn has employed the Shuffle with fine results in the strong Southeastern Conference. The reader is referred to his excellent book *Basketball's Shuffle Offense: A Versatile Pattern for Victory* (Englewood Cliffs, N.J.: Prentice-Hall, Inc., 1960) for a complete picture of the fundamentals and execution of this pattern.

First Step

Be sure you, as the coach, are thoroughly familiar with what you are going to teach. A clipboard, notes or any other helpful crutch will not detract from the intensity of your teaching if you use them discreetly. At any rate, you should know the entire system backwards and forwards before you go on the floor to teach it.

Second Step

Show the entire pattern to your team. Show it on the blackboard and have them walk through it on the floor. Let each team member walk, then run through it from the position he will later play. Be sure each player carries the pattern away from practice with him on paper or in a notebook so that he may study it during his free time. A written test or the threat of one may stimulate some players to greater understanding of the pattern.

Here is the Drake Shuffle in its basic form.

Players #1 and #2 start in guard positions. They are the players who will normally advance the ball into front court. Players #3 and #4 are forwards; #5 is playing a position normally occupied by a center in single post systems. Notice that the center is stationary and high to one side of the key hole lane. The guards are overbalanced to one side of the court. Other than these changes in balance, the setup is the same as for a single post attack.

In the last diagram, all guards are at guard position, forwards are at forward spots and the middle man is back in position,

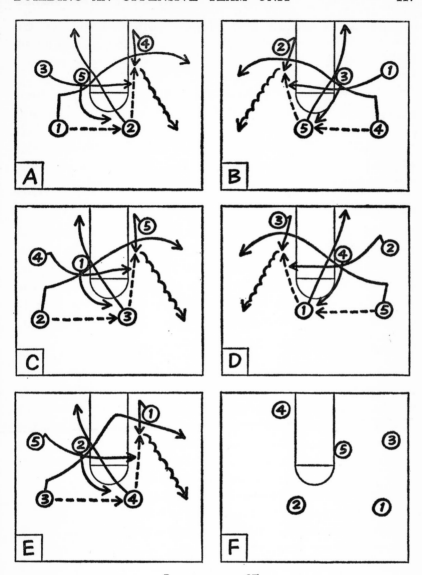

ILLUSTRATION 97.

though none of them are necessarily at their original places. Every player must be able to function at any of the five spots. If the pattern is continued long enough, each man will play each spot, if only for a brief period of time.

Third Step

After you are sure each man is familiar with the pattern, it should be broken down into parts. Each part will receive much practice and supervision. Let every man practice each part, because everyone plays every position at one time or another. Since all players are familiar with the pattern, they will understand the purpose of such specific drills. Here is a part breakdown for practicing the shuffle.

Part One—The Initial Pass. The first pass *must* go to the low post man. The *low post* man is designated as that forward nearest the key hole lane or opposite the stationary post man. The guards may *cue* off the post man. They will get the ball to the forward on the opposite side of the lane from the high post. The pass may go from guard to low post or from guard to guard to low post.

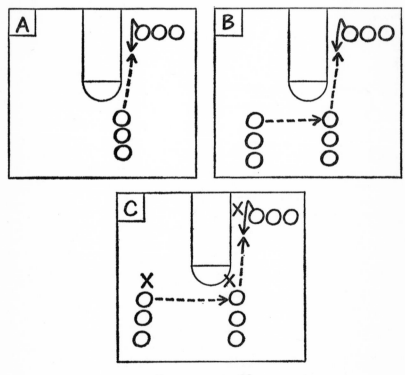

ILLUSTRATION 98.

Here is a drill for practice of this maneuver. After the drill and movements are well learned, put defensive men on passers and receivers. Diagram A shows the ball going from guard to low post, and Diagrams B-C show it going from guard to guard to low post. Notice that the low post fakes and breaks to meet the ball.

Here is the same drill with added defensive men to make receivers and passers work under game conditions.

Part Two—First Cut off High Post. The center or middle man will be designated as the high post. The first cutter is normally a guard, but it may be any of the five at some time during the course of the pattern. Therefore, every man should run this drill. Run it to both sides of the floor. The coach will pass to the first man in a line of low post men. The receiver will pass (bounce pass preferable) to the first cutter from the other line. Note that the cutter fakes one way and cuts opposite, moving close to the

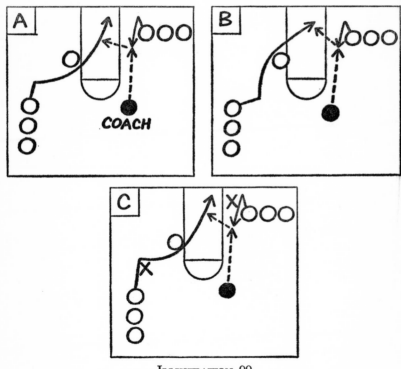

ILLUSTRATION 99.

high post player. He may straight cut or reverse cut. The reverse cut is so named because the cutter goes behind the high post man. His cut in either case should be close, to rub off the defensive man that is playing him.

After the players become proficient in this type of practice, add defensive men to guard low post and first cutters. Here is the same drill with defensive men added. Run both of these drills to the right and left sides of the floor.

Part Three—Second Cut off High Post. The second cutter is always the forward opposite the low post man. He cuts after the first cutter clears the high post man's hip. He should rub tight off the high post in front of the free throw line, or he can fake and reverse cut. The bounce pass is handled easiest. Receivers may jump shoot or drive for a lay-up.

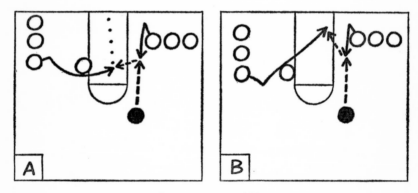

ILLUSTRATION 100.

Here is the same drill with added defensive men to simulate game conditions.

Part Four—Roll-Out by High Post. A line of high post men, a line of low post men, and a line of screeners are necessary to run this drill. The guard passes to a low post man, who passes to the roll-out man. The high post roll-out man will normally wait until he is sure the second cutter is not going to get the pass. If the second cutter should get the pass, the high post man would then become a rebounder. If neither cutter gets the pass, the

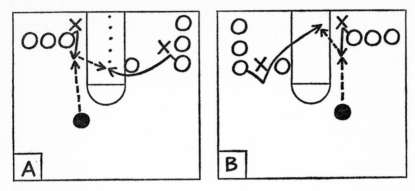

ILLUSTRATION 101.

roll-out man steps out and uses the moving screen to get open. He may set shoot from the head of the circle or continue the pattern if a shot does not materialize. In this drill he will take the shot. Passes to roll-out men may be any kind that can be executed successfully.

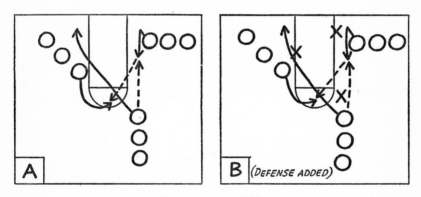

ILLUSTRATION 102.

Part Five—Both Cutters and Low Post Man. The next progression stage combines two parts of the pattern. Part One and Part Two drills are combined. To give them a high post to cut off, station a manager in that position. The coach may pass to the low post line of passers. Run this to right and left sides of the floor.

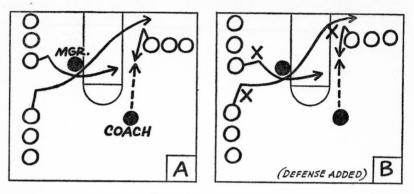

ILLUSTRATION 103.

Part Six—Both Cutters and Roll Out Maneuver. Parts One, Two and Three are combined to form this drill. The coach may stay in the low post and have cutters move on his signal. There is no screen man for the roll-out, but he can time his move as though there were one. Run to both sides of the floor.

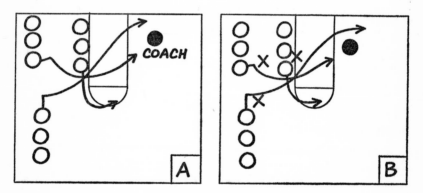

ILLUSTRATION 104.

Fourth Step

After repeated drill on separate parts, your men should be ready to run the entire pattern. Each man will start from the spot you have assigned. There should be no defense to harass them, for they are still learning. In the beginning they will be able to run best the first three options that they have drilled on

in breakdown practice. After they can run those three basic options well, let them continue the pattern for several sequences of
action. Gradually they will learn to run it well from any spot
and with full continuity. At that time they will be ready for the
next progression stage.

Fifth Step

The next step is to add a *passive* defense. Passive means that
the defensive men move with the offensive players but do not
attempt to interfere with passes. Fakes and screens should become a little sharper during this drill. Timing and secondary
positions should be supervised closely. Make each player stick
completely to pattern routes.

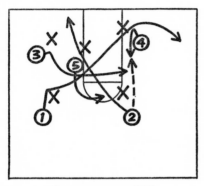

ILLUSTRATION 105.

Sixth Step

Now a full speed defense is added. During full speed defense
practice, allow players to drive for open lay-ups if the defense
"plays the pattern" too much. Use caution in making this con-
cession, because it will turn into a driving drill if you do not. Short
jumps and open sets should be taken just as though a game were
in progress. Greater skill will be necessary in order to make the
crucial pass to the low post man. That pass actually gets the
pattern moving.

Seventh Step

Here is a drill called baskets and losses. It will add the spice
of competition to practice. It also adds some running, for the

defense should be allowed to make a full court break each time
it gains ball possession. A careful record is kept of the number of
baskets the offensive team scores before it has lost ball possession
five times. For that reason, the drill is called baskets and losses.
A loss should count double if the defensive team is able to score
a lay-up on its fast break. If the defensive players do not score
a lay-up, the ball is returned to the offensive team, which attempts to run the pattern again.

Eighth Step

If you desire to add any variations to the pattern, now is the
time to do it. The players have become aware of pattern advantages and disadvantages. Don't make your variations too complicated. You may be destroying one of the advantages, which
is simplicity. The addition of a straight pivot pass from guard to
high post man will keep the defense a little more balanced. A
post split from the strong side or the side that the high post sets
up will also add some offensive versatility to the pattern. There
are any number of variations that you may add. Here are the
two we have mentioned.

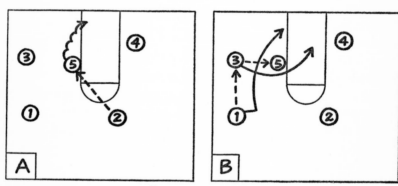

ILLUSTRATION 106.

Ninth Step

Coaches who like the fast break can use it to supplement the
strength of the pattern. They will break down the aspects of
a good fast break and teach it in the same manner that we have

outlined for teaching a pattern. If no shot develops on the fast break, the team will go right into its pattern style offense. Beginners will have a great deal of difficulty maintaining body balance if they attempt a fast break. It is suggested that each player have one or two years experience before the fast break is tried.

Tenth Step

You cannot enter a game without some type of full court game-like practice. It is suggested that you use the clock and put a time limit on the drill before it starts. A ten-minute clock scrimmage, properly officiated, will cause the players to go through early game nervousness, and last-second pressure if the score is close. Vary the length of such scrimmages and do not have one every day. They should be held sparingly, for they are time-consuming and you have many other basketball situations to prepare for. If it is held too often, the players come to resent fundamental practice. Such full court practice should be offered occasionally as a reward for hard work on fundamentals.

TEACHING HINTS

1. Fundamental skills must be acquired before any offense can be run.
2. Free lance systems require the hardest work from the coach.
3. Insist on correct, precise execution every time a movement is performed.
4. Break your system into parts for practice purposes.
5. Put in defensive men and add competition any time it will not be detrimental to the primary purpose of a drill.
6. Be sure you have a defensive "checker" on every shot.
7. Insist that every offensive man go for the rebound unless he is a checker.
8. Try to make your boys believe that the pattern they are running is the best.
9. Breakdown part drill should be continued each day, even after all stages of progression have been passed.

Part III

TEACHING DEFENSIVE SKILLS

9. Man-for-Man Defense

Coaches and teams build *reputations* with offensive systems, but they *win ball games* with good defensive work. Study the champions of past years. Without exception, they are teams that place great emphasis on defense. The "best defense is a good offense" theory has had its day. Strong teams, at all levels of play, are spending more and more time on defense.

Every phase of basketball is subject to fluctuation and variability except defense. Passing, dribbling and shooting may be "on" or "off"; they may be hot or cold. The degree of variability changes from team to team. Size of the playing floor and other physical facilities can affect these skills. Defense is the only *stable element*—the only completely reliable skill in basketball.

Defensive play is appreciated and admired immensely in every team sport except basketball. Good defensive play in basketball gets only passing interest from fans or the press. The press has built good defensive football and baseball players into stars. Outstanding defensive players are just as valuable to a good basketball team, but few basketball players have made all-state, all-conference or all-America because of their defensive prowess. Football and baseball "all-everything" teams, on the other hand, will usually have one or two players who were considered primarily for their defensive ability. We must sell the fans and the press on the value of a good defensive basketball player. We must sell them on the fact that defense is spectacular if one knows what to look for.

Some fans think that any player, even one who is not outstanding physically, can develop into an outstanding defensive man. Nothing could be farther from the truth. Can anyone with courage develop into a good mile runner? To run the mile or to play good defense requires real athletic talent, plus hard work. Possibly the boy who is only average physically can develop into an *adequate* defensive man as the result of hard work. If he is to be truly great, however, he will need all the qualities of the good offensive player. That is one reason why there is no excuse for great offensive players not developing defensively too. Speed, coordination, strength and good reaction are all necessary for either. If these qualities are not present, they must be developed. It is doubtful if innate speed can be increased. This is why boys with poor speed will find it doubly difficult to become great defensive men.

A positive attitude is the first step in teaching defense. A recognition of its value and a strong determination to give this skill its rightful role in practice sessions will help. Many coaches will talk defense at length and appear to know much about it from a technical standpoint. Some of these same coaches fail to put their knowledge to work. They become engrossed in offensive play, and the practice time is over or nearly so before they remember to work on defense.

A positive attitude means that the coach spends a proportionate amount of time on offense and defense. It means that he does not wait until the players are worn out from offensive play before he drills on defense. The defensive drills should be performed immediately after warm-up on certain days to impress the players with its value, since they sometimes have a tendency to rank each drill in importance by the order in which it appears on the practice schedule. Sloppy habits are developed by tired performers. However, players are called upon to perform defensive skills after fatigue in nearly every game. Put defensive practice first, last and in the middle from time to time.

Defensive play must be broken into parts just as offensive play is practiced. Otherwise, the same mistakes will be repeated again and again. Drill on individual skills, such as playing the dribbler, playing the post man, and switching, before attempting to practice as a team.

Defensive Stance

The body position should resemble that of a boxer. Legs should be bent and the feet well spread, with one foot advanced. The defensive player must have balance from front to rear *and* laterally. He must be able to move in any direction. The closer his man gets to him, the more weight will be shifted to the rear foot. At all other times he should strive to maintain an equal amount of weight on both feet. The upper trunk is bent forward at the waist. Both arms are raised with one arm pointed at the ball and the other held wide and low to deflect passes. Marginal vision allows the defensive man to check for possible screeners. He can turn his head a little to look for screeners when he feels that he is in a screening situation.

ILLUSTRATION 107.

Footwork

In moving from one place to another the defensive man should make use of what has come to be known as the boxer's shuffle. To move laterally, he moves first the foot that is nearest his destination. The other foot slides or closes toward the first sliding foot. This action, performed repeatedly, allows a defensive man to move rapidly without crossing his feet. No cross steps should be taken in the front court unless he has lost his man completely and has to run to intercept him.

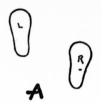

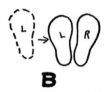

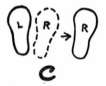

ILLUSTRATION 108.

To move to the rear, the back foot moves first in a slide. The front foot slides back toward it. Be sure the feet are kept spread. It is easy to get them too close together when moving backward or forward. The initial backward move is made easier by first shifting the weight to the rear foot.

To move forward, the first stride is taken with the front foot and the rear foot is pulled up toward it. Again, the feet are kept spread and body weight is balanced.

After the players can perform defensive footwork well, drill them on changing directions rapidly while keeping correct balance. Put all players on the floor and have them move in the direction that you point. Watch their feet. Players who cross their feet during the drill need further instruction. Keep them low and encourage them to use their arms properly.

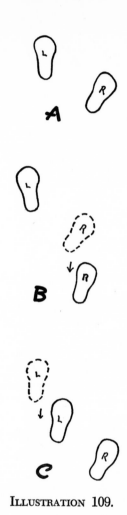

ILLUSTRATION 109.

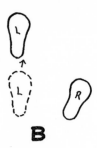

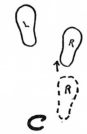

ILLUSTRATION 110.

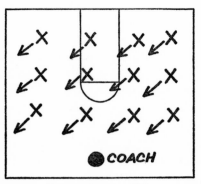

ILLUSTRATION 111.

Guarding Man With Ball

Playing a man who has ball possession is different from guarding one who does not have the ball. If it is in the front court, the defensive man will move in closer to him as the distance to the goal decreases. If his man has not dribbled and is near center line, the defensive player should not get too close. He may drop off two full yards. If his man is in shooting range near the head of the circle or closer, the defensive man must move close enough to prevent a shot. Keep the eyes glued to the ball handler's belt buckle. If he moves, his belt buckle must go with him.

ILLUSTRATION 112.

Guarding a Dribbler

Guarding a clever dribbler is one of the more difficult defensive skills. First of all, a defensive man must not go for a fake dribble and allow his man to get a shot off. The defensive player should watch his man's midsection. If the ball handler takes a step forward, the defensive man must take a step backward with the opposite foot. If he steps sideward, a half step should be taken in that direction with the opposite foot. If it is obvious that the offensive man is going to dribble, a step should be taken with the foot nearest the direction of his drive. *Overplay* him slightly. That is, stay about half the width of his body *ahead* of him. If he is moving laterally to his left, overplay in that direction. By overplaying his move to the left one can be relatively sure that the offensive man is going to be stymied if he keeps moving in that direction. The defensive man can then be alert to a possible reversal of direction. Do not *dig* and *dive* for the ball. Officials are often unable to determine whether or not a foul actually occurs. In most cases they will call a foul anyway.

After halting the dribbler, move in on him and wave the arms vigorously. Try to prevent him from getting rid of the ball until a jump ball is called.

ILLUSTRATION 113.   *Overplay*

Guarding a Man Without the Ball

Once an opponent releases the ball, a defensive player is vulnerable to a cut. Suppose he has moved in close to halt the dribble. If the offensive man gets rid of the ball and cuts quickly, he may "take" the defensive man with the old give-and-go play. As soon as he releases the ball, move back two or more strides, depending on floor position.

When playing a man who does not have the ball, try to see him clearly. Use marginal vision to see the ball at the same time. If it is necessary to lose sight of one or the other, lose sight of the *ball*. Every player should know where his man is at all times. If he is lost for a split second, he may be shooting a lay-up before the defensive man can regain position. Use the arms as an aid. Point at the man with one arm and, with the other, point at the ball.

Keep a good bent-legged stance. The average defensive player
will straighten up as soon as his man gets rid of the ball. That
is what makes him only average. If a defensive man is to be good,
he must stay on defense all the time his team does not have the
ball. While sagging, he may have tailor-made opportunities to
help a teammate out of trouble or to help him double team this
man. Before helping a teammate, the defensive player must make
sure his own man is not moving into a vital area.

ILLUSTRATION 114.

Playing a cutter properly who does not have the ball is a
further indication of defensive skill. Do not *trail* him. It is not
necessary to stay *directly* between him and the basket. Overplay
the angle of his cut. Anticipate his route and destination and
beat him there. If he is allowed to go where he wants, he can
"whip" any defensive player. Overplay him half a man. If he is
breaking into the key hole from a forward spot, break in ahead of
him and try to keep an arm between him and a potential pass.

If a man takes himself out of play by moving deep into a
corner opposite the ball, that opportunity should not be used to
rest. That is the time to be the sixth man on defense. Keep sight
of the resting offensive player at all times and sag off to help
teammates.

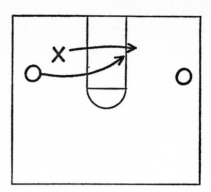

ILLUSTRATION 115.

Guarding the Base Line Driver

The quickest and easiest two points in basketball are gained by driving the base line. Two dribbles, or even one dribble by a skilled man, brings a lay-up, with no opportunity for teammates to help. The main thing, then, is to prevent the initial move of any dribbler down the base line.

Overplay him so that the defensive man is playing on his base line leg, or the leg that is nearest the base line. Don't be a sucker for free throw line fakes and leave him free to go straight to the goal. Keep the leg nearest the base line rearward. On the right side of the floor, the left leg will be back. On the left side of the floor, the right leg will be back. We are designating right and left as though looking at a half court area from mid-floor.

When the defensive man overplays his man, what seems to be plenty of room to drive to the key hole is left open. Knowing that this is the only route left open, the defensive man can be especially alert for just such a move. Further, he has some help from teammates in that area, while there is no one to help if his man goes down the base line.

If the offensive man gets by the defensive man, his only recourse is to try to cut the dribbler off before he gets to the basket. The man on defense should not try to maintain proper footwork. He should go directly to a point about half way to the goal and get directly in front of the opponent. The driver may jump shoot,

ILLUSTRATION 116.

but he may also charge and foul if a courageous position is
maintained.

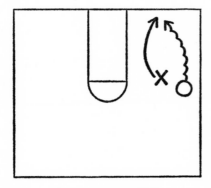

ILLUSTRATION 117.

Guarding the Pivot Man

Every team in the country which uses the single post will attempt to get the ball to him regularly. The post man is near the
goal when he receives. He is usually a tall player. After he receives, he is close without having dribbled. The defensive man
is most vulnerable to fakes. The pivot man is dangerous every
time he gets the ball. The best procedure is, then, to use an ounce

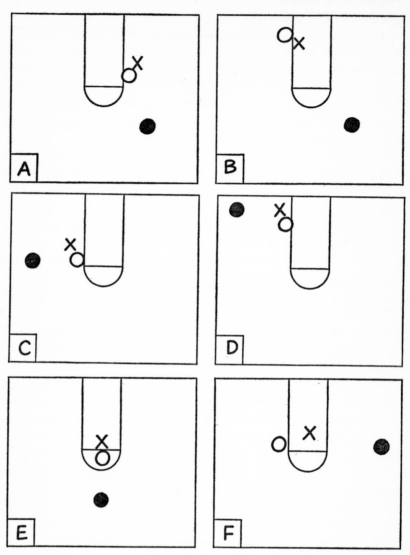

ILLUSTRATION 118.

of prevention and try to keep him from getting the ball.

The primary aim of good defensive pivot play is to keep the ball away from the pivot as much as possible. To do this, the defensive center will station himself between the ball and his man as much as he can afford. This will depend in part on his speed and on the height of the man he is guarding. Assuming he is as fast as the offensive man and as tall, here (Illus. 118) are the positions he will take when the ball is at various points.

As one of our defensive pivot men once told us at half time, "That would all be well and good, coach, if he were nailed to the floor!" It is evident that the offensive man is going to be moving too and that it will not always be possible for your defensive man to maintain these positions.

If he does fail and the post man gets the ball, the defensive post man will move directly between him and the goal and make every effort to prevent a score. Sagging teammates will also be helpful in preventing the post man from receiving. They will also be responsible for helping in many instances after the post man gets the ball. Each of the four other men who is not guarding a man in a critical area should sag toward the middle every time the ball goes there.

Guarding Fake Shots

When an offensive man gets close to the goal, especially if he has not dribbled, the defensive man is open to an assortment of fakes. Here is a good rule of thumb for the defensive man to remember: *prevent the driving lay-up.* Do not give him anything if it can be helped. Remember that the defensive player is already at a disadvantage, however. Do not *leave the floor* on a fake shot. At times the offensive man will get his jump shot. That is much better, percentage-wise, than having him get a lay-up. He will surely get a lay-up or be fouled if the fake is taken. Some coaches insist that every defensive player have *both* feet on the floor at all times except to rebound. That may well be the best solution. If a defensive man leaves the floor on a jump shot, he should be *sure* that the jump shooter's feet have left the floor first.

Switching Techniques

Some good defensive teams switch and some slide. Some teams do both. The main thing is to make up your mind which system you are going to use and to be sure your players understand precisely what you want. Don't leave room for alibis. Don't leave room for doubt and shifting of blame.

Coaches who use switching tactics employ various cues and signals indicating when the switch is on. Sometimes the boy who is in trouble calls it. Sometimes the deep man is always responsible for calling it. Some ball clubs let either man call the switch if he wants to.

We suggest here that if you want to switch, have your boys switch *every* time a close scissors action occurs between two offensive players where the *ball* is involved. If the scissors is *not close,* there is no need to switch. You must show your players over and over what close action is. If the *ball is not involved,* there is no need to switch.

There may be rare exceptions to this rule. If so, adjust to the situation and make the switch automatic even on an unusual play in a particular game. This rule would not affect *pivot cuts* either. It is doubtful if any team switches successfully on pivot cuts. We are speaking of scissors action other than single cuts off the post man. Give your rule of thumb and go into minute detail concerning the exceptions.

It will not be necessary to have one man call the move. Both should call it and assist each other by shoving with their hands vigorously just as they meet during the scissors action. Each player should stay with his own man as long as possible. This will usually result in two defensive players colliding or bumping into each other. As they move together, they will recognize the

ILLUSTRATION 119.

need for switching men. Each will shove his teammate with the nearest hand and call the switch at the same time.

Most switches involve crosses between the guards or between guards and forwards. It is well to practice these particular switches many times. Another occasion that demands alertness of the switching team is that of defensing three-out and two-in offensive formations. Here are four switching drills that will help improve your team in performing the switch technique.

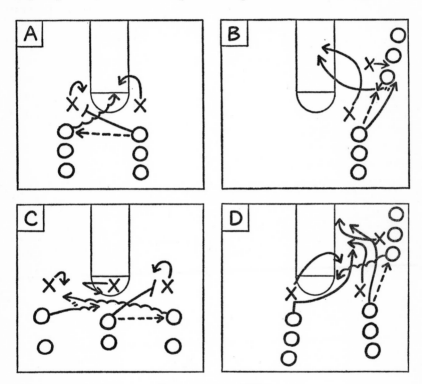

ILLUSTRATION 120.

Switching teams get hurt most by dead screens. The same danger may be presented by deep lateral or side screens and resultant roll-outs and cuts for the basket. In such an event, the cutter has gained an advantage by getting his body between the defensive man and the goal. The defensive man has placed himself in this predicament usually by not being alert. Dead screens should be watched for. Teammates can often warn each other. Experience will indicate to players when they should be most alert for this offensive tactic.

Here are two situations in which the offensive man might gain such an advantage over the switching team.

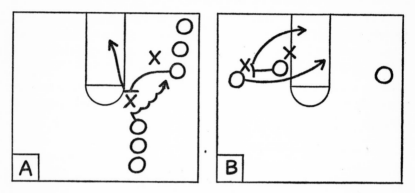

ILLUSTRATION 121.

If the defensive man finds himself in such a dilemma, he has only one recourse. If he is lucky (and he cannot depend on this), a teammate may help him. Otherwise, he should *trail* the offensive cutter toward the goal, holding his hands high over the head of the cutter to prevent him from receiving a return pass.

ILLUSTRATION 122.

He must be careful not to run over the cutter. He must assume that the ball holder is trying to lob a pass to his man. There is no need for him to look backward at the passer. He is in real trouble and should concentrate on preventing his man from receiving a pass for a lay-up. As soon as he possibly can, he must regain normal position on his man.

Of course, the best way to beat screens is to know where they are and to step around them. This knowledge may come from a teammate, or it may come from constant work and drill.

Here is a drill that will help. Station one group of players at random across the floor. Have another group use good defensive footwork and gradually slide through them on signals from the coach.

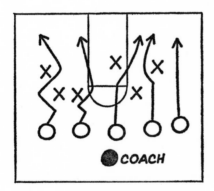

ILLUSTRATION 123.

Playing the Set Shot Over a Stationary Screen

Switching teams have a bit of an advantage defensing this very dangerous play. It occurs when an offensive cutter stops behind the ball handler, receives the ball and sets for a shot over the original ball handler. Here is a common example of this tactic.

The guard is set to shoot over the forward. The two defensive men are behind the original ball handler. They would normally expect the outside man to come around where the switch would occur. Obviously, one of them is going to have to come around the stationary screen if they are to prevent the open shot. If a player comes at him from his left, the potential shooter will drive

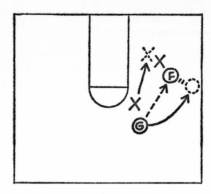

ILLUSTRATION 124.

right. If one comes from his right, he will drive left. There is also the possibility that the screen man will break for the basket at any time. The best defensive move here is simply the lesser of two dangers. The defensive man nearest the ball handler should rush the shooter one step and raise his arm. If, at that instant, the screener breaks, the other defensive man will take him. If the shooter drives left when he is rushed, the other defensive man will take him and the man who rushed will fall back quickly to take the screen man, as in the diagram at the right.

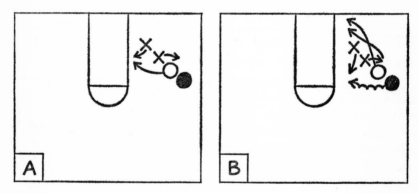

ILLUSTRATION 125.

What happens when a short guard ends up with a tall forward or pivot man? There is only one thing to do. He must guard his man as if his life depended on success until such time that he can *safely* switch back with the player guarding his original man.

To make the switch back, the player guarding the man farthest from the goal or critical area will make the first move. The man guarding the player near the goal must give his entire attention to that man. When his teammate feels he can safely move in and take his man back, he should yell to him and physically shove him out to pick up the man he has left outside. The man nearest the goal cannot be left unguarded for a second. The man outside must be covered again as soon as possible. He should not be left at all if he is involved with action around the ball.

There are many occasions requiring close cooperation between teammates if any good defense is to be devised. Switching calls for more than any other type of defense.

Sliding Techniques

Many fine basketball teams have had great success in the use of a sliding man-for-man defense. They assign each player a man and give him the responsibility for that man, even if "he goes into the lobby."

The greatest advantage of such a policy would be the elimination of excuses or alibis. Each player has exact knowledge of his task. He is to prevent his assigned man from scoring. Of course, he is allowed to help a mate in trouble, but if he cannot, he need not worry as long as he takes care of his own job. Most coaches who believe in the sliding technique point out that, since switching teams have to slide anyway on posts cuts, they might as well learn to slide in every situation. They point to the danger of having little men guarding tall fellows, caused occasionally by switching.

The greatest danger for sliding teams is screening. Close cooperation is needed between team members when an attempt to "pick" one of them occurs. Naturally, the man in the most danger is the one guarding the ball handler. He must be given top priority on floor space when an area becomes congested. Any time his man scissors off a teammate, he must be allowed to come through with him. This means that the man not guarding a ball handler must step *back* to let him pass. The only exception to this rule applies to post cuts. Other exceptions might occur, but they usually result from not being alert or from being already at a disadvantage.

ILLUSTRATION 126.

Sliding practice should be conducted for all of the situations shown in drills for switching teams. The only difference is that the slide is taught instead of the switch.

Playing Post Cuts

Post cuts may be single, double or even triple. Because of multiple cuts executed rapidly and timed to occur at the same instant, sliding is recommended for defensing this offensive move. If the cut is not made tight off a post man, the defensive man should go through, between his two opponents.

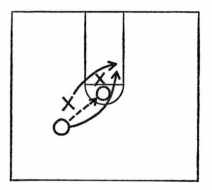

ILLUSTRATION 127.

If the cut is made tight, the defensive man must necessarily go behind the opposing post man to keep from being picked by him. At that second, when he is behind the post man, he is left open for a back-up jump shot by his opponent. He can only console himself here with the fact that a jump shot is less dangerous than a lay-up. The other alternative is to play this situation as switching teams do. When moving behind his teammate guarding the post man, the defensive man must be careful not to help the opposition by screening him with his body. The post could then fake to the cutter and drive opposite, using a screen set by the defense.

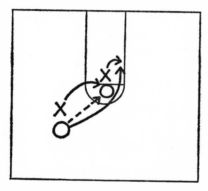

ILLUSTRATION 128.

When a scissors action off a set post man occurs with more than one cutter, the defense is offered the most challenging task in defensive basketball. It is a situation that must be practiced many times to be effective. That is one of the reasons why post men should not be allowed to get the ball if preventing this is at all possible. Every aspect of such a play is loaded with danger for defensive men. Dutch Dehnert of the original Celtics is given credit for originating the pivot crisscross. It is as good today as it was when he first used it.

Here are some situations where daily practice is necessary to prepare your team for defensing multiple pivot cuts. This is the traditional double guard crisscross.

Here is a side post split by one guard and one forward. The pass to the post man may be made by guard or forward. The

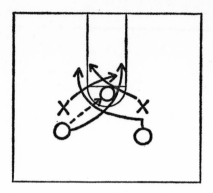

ILLUSTRATION 129.

first cutter can be the passer or his teammate. The defensive man guarding the first cutter should clear through and loosen up, so that he will be sure not to act as a screen against his own team-

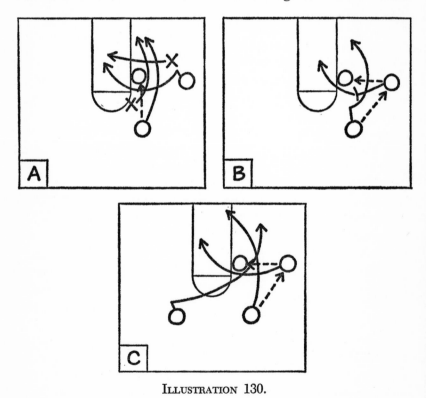

ILLUSTRATION 130.

mate. If the offensive first cutter stops briefly (as is shown in the right diagram) and his defensive man is tight, the guard on the second cutter runs into a double screen set by one opponent and one teammate. He must be able to get between the opposing screen and his teammate's body. He cannot do this if they are standing close together.

Another post cut involves three cutters. The basic moves are the same and the dangers are the same, except that they may be multiplied with the addition of the third man.

Building a *Team* Man-for-Man Defense

Team work is more imperative for a successful defense than it is for a successful offense. Sometimes a better-than-average offense is built around one, two, or three men. An offensive player may be rather successful with no help from any of his teammates. The offensive players have an advantage to start with. They have the ball. They can fake, shoot, pass or any number of things that the defensive team must be ready for. They know what they are going to do while the defense is strictly in a guessing situation. Therefore, the offensive team has an advantage. The defensive team has its back to the wall. Defensive teams must pull together. Each man must cooperate or none will reap any rewards.

A good defense draws team members closer together quicker than anything the coach could ever dream of as a morale-building device. There is much courage involved in playing tough defense. Displays of courage are not hard to find. The player who stands unflinchingly in front of a strong, hard driver may have to recover his teeth after he gets up. He will also have a free throw coming. The would-be athletes will not make this sort of play often. It is the sort that stimulates and fires a team to pull together against a common opponent. The new charging-blocking rule has given defensive teams a strong boost by allowing them to get in front of the driver whenever they can.

It takes moral and physical courage to play good defense. When one is tired, he may try to take his rest while on defense. Of course, if a player *thinks* he is tired, he may not be. He must eliminate false feelings of fatigue and dig in harder to do his best. If he is truly tired, however, there is nothing for him to do except volunteer to be removed from the game. A tired player cannot play defense.

The courageous ball club—the ball team with good teamwork—is a team with great pride. It is a team whose individuals vie for the honor of guarding the opposing team's top player. It is a team where each man is unhappy if he is not given this assignment. It is a ball club where the most coveted trophy is the "best defensive player" award. A team with such spirit, with such pride, with such courage will be hard to beat. Every single one of these qualities can be developed by playing good defense.

The first step in building strong defense is practice on individual skills. These skills have been analysed and illustrated. Constant drill is necessary to develop them, just as constant drill is necessary in order to learn to pass well. After all these skills can be performed well, the coach is ready to bring his players together to develop *team* man-for-man defense.

A number of tactics reveal a team as one that is well coached and well drilled on defense. Let's take a look at some of these tactics and discuss each.

1. *"Talk" Defense.* A good defensive ball team will sound like a very spirited baseball infield. They constantly pep each other up with lively chatter and talk. They warn each other of screens, call switches and switch backs. Such tactics are psychologically disconcerting to opponents. It is so encouraging to teammates that they do not have the "guts" to loaf on such hard-working fellow players.

2. *"Stick" the Ball.* To stick the ball is to get right in the "throat" of the man who has it. It can be dangerous to get that close to a man if there is not close cooperation between team members. It leaves you more open to drives, fakes or screens. It also makes it difficult for the opponent to pass or shoot. The teams that do not employ sagging defenses might not be able to use this tactic. If every player is sagged off except when his man has the ball, the boy guarding the ball can rely somewhat on the sagging players for help if he gets in trouble.

3. *Sagging and Sinking.* A good sagging team sticks the ball hard while everyone else sags off toward the middle and the goal.

Of course, the defensive post man must maintain an advantageous position on his man at all times. Actually, he has less to worry about with a good sag defense because it is difficult to pass to the post spot. Every man should have *both* arms up. Each person should have his arms up if he is on the opposite side of the floor from the play. Ten arms can present a strong psychological, if not physical, barrier to a passer.

Sinking teams look much like a zone defense. They don't stick the ball handler unless he gets in close to the head of the circle. They will give away a few shots from the outside in order to cut out everything by way of open shots inside or close to the basket. We will show good positions for every man on a team using the sagging man-for-man defense. Notice that the man on the ball handler is close. His teammates should be talking to him, warning him of screens, encouraging him. If his man gets rid of the ball, he becomes a sagger, a talker, an encourager of the others. These diagrams show a sagging defense working against a single post offense. The relative positions and principles can be applied to any type offense. These positions would be good whether a team used switching or sliding techniques. The dark offensive circle indicates the man with the ball.

All of the defensive post positions are not shown here. The defensive man should endeavor to play as much to the side or front of his man as he can. If his man plays a low post position, the defensive man will play in front of him. Off side sag and good arm movement by the defensive post man will help dispel some of the danger from lob passes. The last diagram shows the offensive post man on the opposite side to the ball. This is possibly the only occasion that the defensive post man will have to sag. Even so, he must be much aware of his man.

4. *Picking up Loose Cutters.* No matter how hard a team works, a man will get free occasionally. He may be a dribbler or a cutter without the ball. Any defensive player near the goal and near the cutter should "co-op" on such a free man until the man originally guarding him can get back in position. If the free man is about to score a lay-up, the man helping should leave his man completely to prevent the sure two points. If the free man is not in position to hurt his team too much, the co-op man will sag

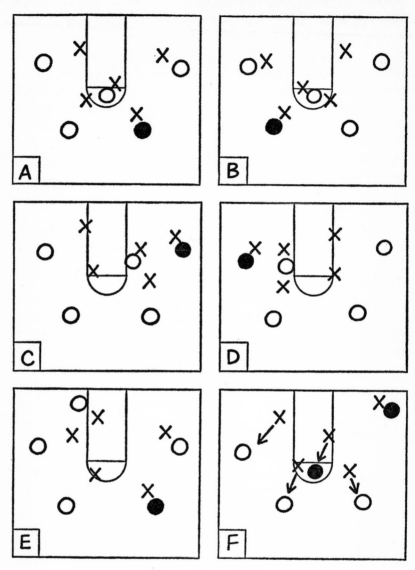

ILLUSTRATION 131.

toward him, maintaining the best possible position on his man. In other words, he will not leave his man completely but will play both men for the moment. This sort of judgment requires hours of work and a good attitude toward defense. It is the sort of thing that teams with good teamwork do. It is the sort of thing that separates great teams from good teams. Sometimes a co-oping team man can get a charging foul called if he steps directly and unflinchingly in front of a free cutter. If this occurs, he has transformed a negative situation into a positive play in a split second. Such a play "lifts" a team to greater effort, and such a man is more valuable to a team than any offensive player can ever be.

5. *Co-oping On Post Men or "Hot Shots."* The best way to prevent a pivot man from scoring is to keep him from getting the ball. The sag diagrams already shown indicate good position for accomplishing this mission.

If the post man should get the ball, any defensive guard whose man is not in a critical position at the time should peel off on the post man like an angry hornet. There could be a situation where every man on the floor is playing the post man if only with one hand. They would simply back off toward the middle and reach in toward him with one hand and keep the other arm pointing at their own man to remind themselves of their first responsibility. Here is such an extreme situation.

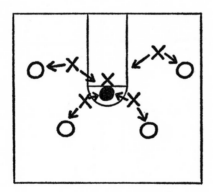

ILLUSTRATION 132.

It is more than likely that only one team member will be able to help the defensive post man. At any rate, any help at all is better than none. Those men who sag in to help should keep main vision on their own men. By use of marginal vision they can help

the defensive post man with one arm. This one-arm extension
into the middle is disconcerting to the ball receiver if it doesn't
actually deflect a pass or dribble. Here is a more realistic situation
of co-oping on the post man.

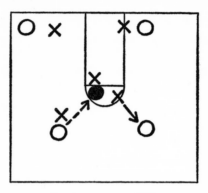

ILLUSTRATION 133.

6. *Blocking Out Rebounders.*   The technique of positioning
for rebounding has already been illustrated in the chapter dealing
with rebounding and tipping. Good team work on the defensive
board calls for all five men (not just the man guarding the
shooter) to get into proper position to rebound. Even the guards
will come up with more rebounds than might be imagined. They
will get some off the boards and some will rebound wide to them
if they are alert and in good position.

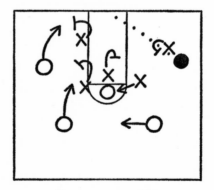

ILLUSTRATION 134.

TEACHING HINTS

1. Defense wins games—offense wins reputations.
2. Defense must be "sold" to the fans and the press.
3. Teach defensive parts or skills before conducting team drills.
4. A defensive man is important to the team even if his man doesn't have the ball.
5. Overplay the direction of dribblers and cutters.
6. Whether a player switches or slides is unimportant—just be sure the others know what to expect.
7. Don't let your learning get ahead of your doing. Many people *know* a lot about defense; few actually *teach* it.

Part IV

TEACHING SPECIAL SKILLS

10. Zone Defense

A good number of fine basketball coaches rebel at the thought of using a zone defense. Professional teams are not allowed to use it in their leagues. It is said that the zone defense causes a lack of fan interest. Some coaches feel that it creates development of lazy habits among their players.

The majority of these reasons are advanced because the old-fashioned method of playing zone defense created such attitudes. At one time the zone was the lazy player's method of defending. Five men congregated around the goal and allowed the opposition to blast away with free outside shots. Such a defense traded the outside shot for an absence of any type of shot inside. The offense could have no effective pivot play and no drives for the goal.

Unfortunately, this type of zone is still being used by some teams. There is a new and different kind of zone defense that is worthy of the best basketball teacher's use. It is an aggressive defense. It does not trade or give away outside shots to protect the inside. This zone defense doesn't intend to give away free shots inside or outside. It is this pressure-type, aggressive, tough zone defense that we will discuss in this chapter. All the principles advanced here should not be associated with the teaching of lazy defense of any structure. If these principles are followed and properly taught, your opponents will be surprised to find that you are not *giving* them the outside shot. They will be surprised to learn that you are not giving them anything.

No matter what formation you use, there are certain basic principles that should be followed. These principles may be called policies that your players will put into effect. Your boys should be taught these policies and taught to recognize the value of each.

1. Getting back in time to defend

The very first objective is to get the team back in time to defend. The zone defense is *supposed* to be weak against a fast break offense. The best weapon against an offensive fast break is a *defensive fast break*. All offensive series should have one or two players designated as checkers at various stages of the series. Nevertheless, all five men have to get downfloor, and get there immediately, after ball possession is lost. They should get downfloor faster than they would go to the offensive end of the floor. If a team fast breaks, they must do this and maintain possession of the ball. This means they cannot run as they can ordinarily run on a dash. As a defensive team, they can run even faster, because they do not have to maintain good balance. If a team does not fast break on offense, they have all their energy left for the defensive fast break. There is *no excuse* for an offensive team getting a lay-up before the defense is set.

The first man down should halt the dribbler. The second man down takes the second position behind him. This is a good policy whether you play man-for-man defense or zone defense. Of course, the first man down would protect the goal if there is a potential receiver standing under it.

2. Playing the ball

Old-fashioned zones did not put a great deal of pressure on the ball handler. The aggressive method makes a radical departure from such a policy. When an offensive team moves into front court, it should meet resistance immediately. The stance of the player guarding the ball should be *wider* (for the feet) and *closer* (for the body) than that for the man-for-man stance. The stance is wider because it will make a dribbler go wider, or about half a step farther, to get around the defensive man. It should be closer because he is not particularly unhappy if the man does dribble around him. The dribbler must go wide, and if he doesn't, he may charge and foul. If the dribbler gets around the first man, another defensive player will pick him up. The primary purpose of the defensive man playing the ball is to cause the ball handler to make a poor pass. He gets in close to the ball handler, in a wide stance, and moves his arms in a windmill fashion. He does not try to steal the ball and is careful not to foul. He wants to deflect the ball or cause the passer to throw *high*. A high pass is anybody's ball. The defensive players in a zone formation should be especially alert for high passes or those that have been deflected.

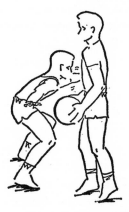

ILLUSTRATION 135.

3. Playing position away from the ball handler

Those players not playing the ball handler should not congregate immediately behind him. They should back off and spread out as much as possible. If an offensive man is near the ball handler, it may be necessary to stay close. If there is no other offensive man close, each defensive man should float until he reaches an area where an offensive man is a potential receiver. He should play to intercept the passes to possible receivers.

A good zone will create five-on-one situations on rare occasions. There should always be three on one. That is, there should be three men in a line between the ball handler and the goal. When offensive men are poorly spaced, it could conceivably become four or five on one.

A zone defensive player should never get directly under the goal. He cannot rebound from there. If an offensive player gets behind the goal, he has taken himself out of contention and there is no need to guard him.

4. Overplay the passer and pass receivers

While the man-for-man defense is concerned with overplaying the dribbler, the zone is aimed primarily at overplaying the passer or receivers. By the nature of your formation, players can anticipate the direction of a coming pass. The player guarding the passer should take about half a step to block the anticipated pass. His teammate nearest the potential receiver will take half a step in front of the receiver. The objective is to prevent free movement of the ball. It is a method of deflecting and intercepting passes. It will cause an offense to deviate from its intended passing formations.

5. Defensing the pivot area

A zone defense is easily beaten if the pivot is not protected. The first objective is to keep the ball out of that area. If a pass is made into the middle, all five defensive men will slough toward the ball to make it difficult for the ball handler to pass or shoot well.

6. Team arm action

To get the three-on-one situations consistently, every man must keep an alert stance and keep both arms up. If each man keeps his arms up, more passes will be made in a high floating manner. Floating passes will not beat a zone. The knees should be kept bent at all times so that a player can move instantly for an interception of a high or deflected pass. If the offense is forced to throw high passes, they are at a grave disadvantage. This disadvantage is enhanced by consistently good arm action of all five players.

These six principles will hold true no matter what type of zone is used. There are numerous formations to choose from. Player personnel, opposition and other factors will help you determine your formation. Some basic formations are 1-3-1, 2-1-2, 2-3, 3-2 and 1-2-2. We are going to take one and suggest a procedure for teaching it. The same procedures can be used even if you select

a formation other than the sample type given here. We will show
the 1-3-1 and one procedure for teaching it. We will assume that
all of the fundamental principles have been strongly instilled in
each player.

Here is the basic formation that gives the 1-3-1 defense its
name. It is only a starting formation, because as soon as the offense
crosses center line, the 1-3-1 will shift to meet it. This formation
changes every time the ball moves even slightly. Three players
are in line from side line to side line. Three are in line from center
court to goal. The free throw line is used to key the lateral line
on its position.

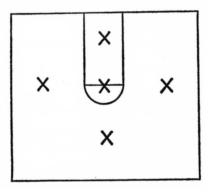

ILLUSTRATION 136.

There are five spots that each player must recognize and react
to automatically. The first one is directly in front of the goal and

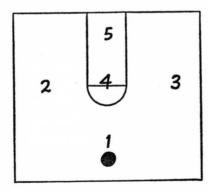

ILLUSTRATION 137.

may be anywhere from center line to the free throw line. If the ball is in that area, the #1 man takes the man and the other players maintain basic positions, unless there is a receiver to overplay.

Another spot that is defended by reflex action is the right wing position. The defensive wing player, #3 on the right side, will overplay the pass to the corner. This half step overplay also discourages a dribble by the ball handler. There are not three men in precise alignment with ball and goal. #4 is directly in line, but #2 is in his secondary position and #5 has started to cheat toward the corner in case the ball is passed there. #1 has floated to the free throw line to help clog the pivot area.

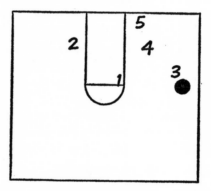

ILLUSTRATION 138.

The right corner is defended by #5. He has already cheated a little in that direction, but if the ball does get to the corner, he moves to guard that man strongly. #3 overplays a possible return pass to the wing, so that a high, long pass out to the front must be made. In that case, #1 should be alert to intercept it. #4 has taken the second position, and #2 has moved all the way in to a spot one yard in front of the goal. If the ball is passed to a corner, the offensive team should be stymied right there. It should never be allowed to get the ball out successfully.

The left wing defensive position is slightly different from the right wing, since #4 plays the left corner. Too much burden is

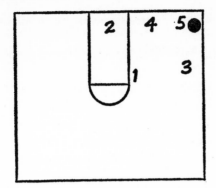

ILLUSTRATION 139.

placed on #5 if he has to play both corners. To alternate their assignments strengthens both positions, but it also causes each side of the floor to be played slightly differently. #2 overplays the ball handler, #4 cheats one step toward the corner, #1 has the free throw line, #3 is moving toward the basket and #5 has moved one step toward the corner, since he will take the second spot if the ball does go to the corner.

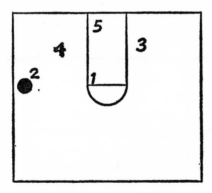

ILLUSTRATION 140.

The left corner is also played differently from the right corner. #4 plays the ball handler, #5 takes the second spot and #3 has the goal. #2 overplays the pass out, and #1 moves even closer to the middle. If a high long pass is made to get the ball out of the corner, every one of the five defensive men moves and moves fast enough to recover his original position. #1 goes for the interception. The men know they are going back to their original positions because they will not allow the ball to be passed to the middle or back out to a wing spot.

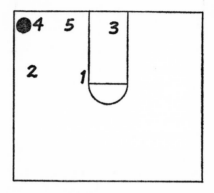

ILLUSTRATION 141.

There are two other positions that will have to be dealt with. One is the middle or post area. The ball should not be allowed to go there often. If it does, the middle man will guard the ball handler strongly and every other defensive player will sag toward the middle and the goal at the same time.

The point or #1 man plays the ball any time it is out front. If there are two players out there passing the ball back and forth, the point man is put at a disadvantage. In that event, he will play only one of them while the offside wing man will come up as far as an imaginary line drawn across the floor from side line to side line and intersecting the head of the circle. The point man will play the man who is adjacent to the greatest accumulation of offensive strength. That is, he will play the man on the strongest side of the floor. The #5 and #4 men will *flex* just a little, as is shown in the diagram. These adjusted positions are held only as an initial position. As soon as the ball moves, regular or normal 1-3-1 positions will be taken. Wing men will never come higher or farther out than the dotted line.

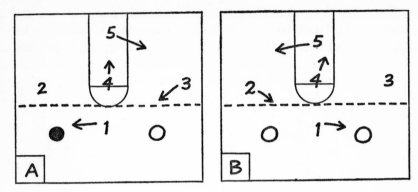

ILLUSTRATION 142.

1-3-1 Personnel Assignments

The point or #1 player should indeed be the team's number one defensive player. He should be fast, intelligent and a leader. He is a person who constantly harasses the opposition. Usually this man will be a guard. #1 has five basic positions to play. He should be drilled as an individual on these positions. The coach can put him at each spot and tell him the spot number. The coach can then stand at center court and call these numbers as signals. Here are the five primary spots. There will be other points for him to cover, but these five should be automatic for him. The open circle is the ball and the dark circle is #1. The numbers are his signals.

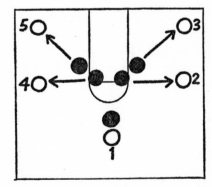

ILLUSTRATION 143.

The wing men, #2 and #3, should be drilled together. They have an equal number of positions to play. Here are the wing men, their primary positions for each spot and signals for each.

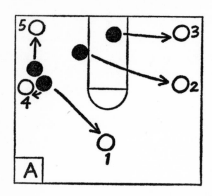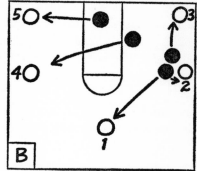

ILLUSTRATION 144.

Note that on signals 1, 4 and 5 each man keeps his normal wing spot. That is the biggest reason why your slowest men can be put at the wings. They are the easiest to play and require the least speed. If the team has a couple of boys who are otherwise pretty good basketball players but who lack speed for man-for-man defense, this zone might well be the defense for that team.

Player #4 should be the second best team defensive player, or first among the taller players. He has five positions to cover and he has a long way to travel in covering them. He must be

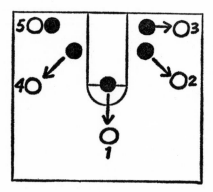

ILLUSTRATION 145.

fast, and he should be one of the taller players. Here are his spots and signals.

The goalie is usually your tallest player and the best rebounder. He is the second best big defensive player. The weakest guard and the weakest forward are usually put at the wings. The best tall man and the next best tall man are put at the middle and goalie positions. Your goalie should be in position to get the most rebounds. The wing men actually get more rebound opportunities than might be suspected of their second and third positions. The goalie need not be an exceptionally fast man. Here are his positions and signals. Players #4 and #5 might be drilled, on occasion, as a two-man drill.

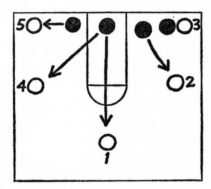

ILLUSTRATION 146.

After the players can cover these basic spots by reflex action, they need to work on the spots that could be termed "infrequent." Defense for pivot play is infrequent because the ball should not be allowed to get in there very often. The spots on either side of #1 are played only infrequently because most teams will run a one-man front offense against a one-man front defense. Even so, these spots must be faced on occasion. They need not present a great problem. It is suggested that the coach *take* the ball to these spots and work all five men as a team. Each man will have to flex slightly out of the normal four or five spots he usually has to play. He should consider it a gift when, in a game, a team takes the ball to one of his four or five regular spots. The number will vary according to position. Some players have an extra spot to play, as in the case of the middle man, #4. It is suggested that you have a five-man drill of *regular* positions and a five-man drill of *infrequent* positions. They may be called Drills One and Two, or any name you want to give them.

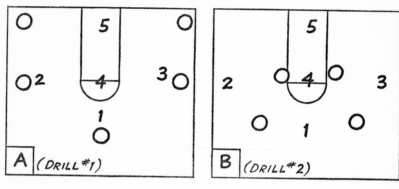

ILLUSTRATION 147.

TEACHING HINTS

1. It is better to teach one type of zone well than to attempt several in a haphazard manner.
2. Teach aggressive zone play. Give 'em nothing, anywhere, any time.
3. Zone defense is not the defense for a lazy coach or team.
4. Stance is closer and feet are wider than in the man-for-man defense.
5. Overplay the passer and pass receiver. Don't allow them to move the ball freely.
6. Overplay the pivot. Do not allow the opposition to move the ball to that spot easily.
7. Don't congregate. Stay spread if there is no necessity of playing close to the man guarding the ball handler.
8. Never take a defensive position under or behind the goal. You are out of play.
9. Fast break on defense. There is no excuse for any good defensive team giving its opposition a lay-up.
10. Do not give them the outside shot.

11. Be specific in teaching a zone defense. It's not *what* formation you use but *how* you teach it.
12. Make personnel assignments according to position and abilities.

11. Jump Ball Skills

The thorough basketball teacher must organize practice to cover every game time situation. Practice of the jump ball is one of them. Jumps occur from 10 to 15 times each game. The percentages could swing heavily in favor of the team that consistently controls the tap. Ball possession is worth points. Even if a team gets the ball only one time more than its opponent, that margin could be adequate for victory.

We cannot assume that the taller boy will get the tap. Intelligence and timing play a vital role in determining which team will get the ball. Even if the taller man makes the tap, it is still free for anyone who can get it. It is even possible that small, quick players have an advantage, at least as far as receiving the tap is concerned. The lack of height on a ball club is no excuse for neglecting practice of jump ball situations.

A team that has a preponderance of short players should concentrate on drills designed to intercept a tapped ball. If the team has a good number of tall players, they will want to practice for offensive breaks or sure possession of seemingly sure taps.

Be sure to keep a record of the times your team gets possession. If you have short men and equal your opposition in taps received, you have turned a negative factor into one that is positive. If you have tall men and equal your opposition in number of taps secured, the team has not fully utilized its advantage.

The Jump

Height of the toss for jumps varies from league to league. Each team should try to learn the rule of thumb being used in its area.

174

Some regions will ask the officials to toss the ball three feet above the taller man's head. It is not known or understood how officials are supposed to be able to toss so precisely. Nor has anyone been able to determine what the short man is to do during the jump. He might as well lead the band, for under such a system he will surely not get an opportunity to jump. Nevertheless, various conferences have such methods.

The rule book states that the ball is to be thrown higher than either man can jump. Of course, there is no way to determine exactly how high two players can jump simply by looking at them. If the ball is thrown strongly into the air, however, both men will have to tap it on its downward flight. Timing and practice will be of more significance. Check with your officials from time to time to find out how they are tossing for jumps. Your practice sessions should then be held to conform to the methods used in the games.

Most boys will be able to tap better and more accurately with their strong or natural hand. A right hander will want to turn his right side to his opponent in preparation for the jump. Some boys have been successful at tapping with the offside hand. If they turn the right side, they twist during the jump and tap with the left hand, or vice versa. For beginners, the right side for right handers, the left side for left handers is the best teaching policy.

The feet should be spread about shoulder width or less. An extremely wide base does not help when height is desired. The wide base is necessary for balance. We are more concerned here with utilization of all the strength in both legs for the spring. One foot may be slightly forward. For right handers, this will usually be the right foot. A low crouch, with weight distributed evenly on each foot, helps gain full use of both legs. The trunk should not bend forward much, since the jump will be made with the legs. The head and eyes are focused upward on the flight of the ball. The arms are at either side of the knees. Some boys can utilize some of the swing-up motion and like to pull the arms slightly rearward.

It is not necessary to swing the whole arm into the ball. The strength of the fingers, hand and wrist is all that need be used. The tapping arm should be extended straight upward. Some tap-

ILLUSTRATION 148.

pers strike the ball too hard for good receiving and some do not tap it strongly enough for control. The ball should be tapped firmly, high and to the outside of the intended receiver. Outside is designated as offside from his nearest opponent.

In executing the jump and tap, the offside arm should not be brought up. A higher jump can be made with one arm than with two. If only one arm is extended the shoulder can be raised on that side. This results in an extra two or three inches on the height of the jump.

The eyes should be concentrating on the ball and the motion used in tossing it. If the toss is made higher than either boy can jump, be cautious of jumping too soon. If the toss is low and quick, be ready to go with the official's arm. Timing is extremely important. *Always jump.* If the opponent is nine feet tall and your jumper is only five feet tall, have him jump anyway. Poor timing by the opponent or good timing by your man may result in a demoralizing blow to the opponent.

There are a number of good drills that will help players learn the right amount of force needed to control the ball. Let each man tap repeatedly against a wall, with a strong jump preceding each tap. Have them pair off and tap back and forth to each other at a distance of five or six feet. Run competitive jump ball drills, so that they will learn to tap high and wide, away from the opponent.

ILLUSTRATION 149.

Receiving the Tap

The procedure for catching a tapped ball will depend upon the objective of the team. Some teams desire only to gain possession, while others try to create fast break opportunities or scoring situations out of jumps. We will discuss here receiving for possession only.

Receivers can get into the circle after the ball is touched by either jumper. The first objective is to cut the opponent out of the picture entirely by stepping between him and the tap. The tap should be made to the hand that is away from his opponent. If he has to jump for the tap, he has even greater insurance. A twist similar to that used in rebounding will enable him to get his body between the ball and his opponent.

Do not allow receivers to catch with *one hand*. Both hands should grasp the ball just as in rebounding or catching a hard pass. Many times the receiver will get a bump or jostling motion from the opposition. If he does not have both hands on the ball or if the bumping comes when his hand first touches the ball, possession will be lost.

ILLUSTRATION 150.

Team Position for Jumps

There are three basic approaches to the jump ball. Some teams may *desire ball possession* only. Others intend to *score* directly from the tap. A team may choose to *defend* its front court against an extremely tall team. Any of these objectives may be used at any of the jumping circles. We will consider all three objectives for jumping at center court.

If an opponent has several very tall men, you might well elect to defend strongly and prevent a scoring move by the opposition. Here is a formation calculated to give you the best and surest defense in such cases. It is designed strictly to prevent the lay-up drive from a tap.

The first player in this tandem formation will attempt to stop the ball from advancing until all five men can get into their regular defensive positions. If the ball should advance past the first man, the number two or deep man will be there as a safety checker.

If a team considers its jumping ability equal to that of the opposition, it may elect to try for ball possession. Receiving and tapping methods already analysed should be followed.

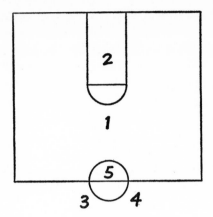

ILLUSTRATION 151.

When attempting ball possession, never allow two opponents to stand side by side. The jumper is thus given a tailor-made opportunity to tap the ball between two such men, with there being little chance for an interception.

The average player can tap best in the direction toward which he is facing. He can tap almost equally well to either of the men he faces if the formation is the traditional alignment. He cannot tap quite so well to the front man opposite, and he is weakest tapping to the back man, #4, opposite his line of vision.

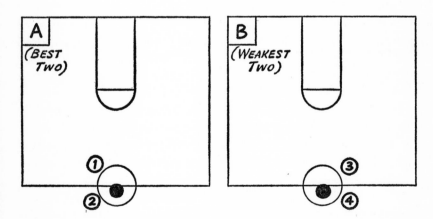

ILLUSTRATION 152.

This diagram is drawn under the assumption the tapper is righthanded and is facing the left side of the floor. The degree of tapping ease is ranked, 1-4, as these players are numbered. Therefore, the man adjacent to #4 can assume safely a great percentage of the time that his man will not receive the tap. He can be a sort of free agent to intercept. His calculated gamble gives his team four receivers to his opponent's three. Percentages are much higher in favor of his team. If the tapper is a left hander, #2 would become the free agent. If a tapper uses the twist and offside hand tap method, he will actually be tapping toward the free agent. Therefore, this system would have to be discarded immediately.

If the team has a decided height advantage for the jump, you may elect to pre-designate a receiver in deep back court or at a side line. This is almost a sure method if the receiver will not telegraph or receive from the same spot every time.

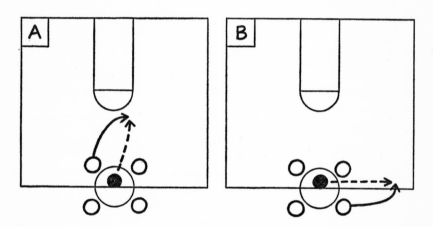

ILLUSTRATION 153.

Three basic principles may be applied if the jump is at any of the three circles. If the jump occurs in an opponent's front court, an extra danger is present. A tap there can result in a goal more easily and quickly than at the other two circles. Extra precautions must be taken. One precaution is to be sure that your two taller men line up nearest the goal for defensive measures. That area from the free throw line to the goal must be protected first. The free agent would certainly help in that direction. In taking his position, each man will want to line up so that he can get his defensive position quickly, especially if the opposition has the advantage of the jump. Even if you have an advantage, it is too dangerous to have every team member breaking with the tap. One or two men should be designated as checkers or insurance agents.

TEACHING HINTS

1. Do not assume that you will get the ball every time you have the height advantage.
2. Turn sideward to the jumping opponent and tap with the natural hand.
3. Tap firmly but so that the receiver can handle it.
4. Tap with the fingers, hand and wrist.
5. Receiving is as important as tapping. The tap without the ball is of no consequence.
6. Do not get into the circle until the ball has been touched by one of the jumpers.
7. Receive with both hands.
8. Determine the least likely man to receive on each jump.
9. Be especially cautious of jump situations at the opponent's goal.
10. Make sure you are well protected against scoring maneuvers from center court when the opponents have a decided height advantage.

12. Ball Control Techniques

Some people prefer to use the words ball possession instead of ball control. "Freeze" is a word that seems to indicate that a shot will not be made under any circumstances. All too often, the word denotes exactly what the players do when trying to maintain ball possession. After playing a fast-paced game for three and one-half quarters, they are often unable to change to the slow possession kind of game demanded by most freezing procedures.

If the freeze is started too soon, players may choke. The defense may have time to become familiar with the system being used and to cope with it better as the freeze goes on. If the freeze is started too late, there is the possibility that your team will win anyway. It is assumed that a freeze is to be used by the team that is leading in point production late in a game.

Use a method that offers scoring opportunities. A system that doesn't even threaten to shoot will not last long. Scoring opportunities will keep the defense honest and allow the offensive team to "fatten up" the lead they already have. Since the defensive team is behind in the score, they will be gambling and making mistakes that can be used by the freezing team. The freezing team should not gamble. They are winning and should remember that. There is no need to take shots that are not extremely high percentage shots. They have the ball and the lead. They should control the ball and the game. They are in the driver's seat.

A freeze system, no matter how sound, cannot be successful if the fundamentals of the game have not been well learned. Sound fundamentals and cool, poised players can utilize a freeze method to "pour on the steam." They can capitalize on each mistake the opposition makes. Poise is a trait possessed only by skilled and experienced players. Some boys will develop poise much earlier than others. A junior high or high school player may be much cooler under fire than a college player. It can be developed. Much practice in pressure situations will prepare the athlete and give him a feeling of confidence, which results in a poised performance at game time.

There are certain rules of thumb that should be constantly stressed when teaching a freeze system. As basketball progresses and various teams become successful using all types of offense and defense, one becomes more and more reluctant to use the words *never* and *always*. Yet our teaching must be positive, even if in later years a method proves to be wrong or not the best method. I am convinced that a method that is completely unsound, yet taught in a positive and confident manner, will be more successful than a sound method taught in a negative and unsure manner. The principles listed here have been sound for many years, and it is believed that they will be sound for many more years. Teach them in a confident manner. Use them with complete assurance.

1. Stay out of danger areas

Any area adjacent to a line is dangerous. The line acts as an additional defensive man. The offensive player cannot move in that direction. The line thwarts him as much as a defensive man would. Stay at least three feet from all boundary lines. The corners are doubly dangerous. If an offensive player gets into a corner, one defensive man and the two lines intersecting create a three-on-one situation. If two defensive men get on the ball handler and he is in a corner, he has voluntarily created a four-on-one situation. These odds are all in favor of the opposition and add up to nothing more than a gift of the ball when you have tough opponents. Of course, the three-second area will be avoided like the plague. A three-second violation during a freeze is most demoralizing, because it is useless. Team members who are working hard feel a letdown when a foolish mate lingers too long and simply gives the ball away.

2. Don't offer double team opportunities

Try to develop a system that does not allow two offensive players to cross any time the ball is controlled by one of these two players. Players may crisscross as much as they like as long as neither of them has the ball. The best double team opportunities are afforded where crossing maneuvers are attempted by two men, one of whom has the ball.

3. Don't allow cross-court passes

An interception of a cross-court pass is like a flat pass interception in football. There is usually no one in a position to prevent a quick, easy score by the interceptor. Cross-court passes can be timed for interception easier than short passes. They are usually long passes, but while a long pass can be completed easier than a cross-court pass, it can be dangerous. A long pass belongs to anybody who can get it. The defense has the same right to the ball as the offense.

A defense working against a freeze will be looking for these two types of passes. They should be avoided. No matter what type of pass is used, be sure that every pass receiver comes to *meet the pass*. His fakes and breaks to receive should be more strenuous than usual. Instruct passers not to throw to teammates who are not moving toward them.

4. Allow little or no dribbling

There was a time when one clever dribbler could conduct a freeze by himself. There are still teams who depend completely on one man to freeze the ball when it is necessary. There will be teams in the future who may successfully use such a method. We will speak here of the average young team that has not such an outstanding player. Even the team with a good dribbler should consider that if the outstanding athlete is ill and unable to play in a game where the freeze is needed, that team will have a long bus ride home.

A sound method that does not depend on one man offers more insurance for the long haul. Even the outstanding dribblers are finding it more and more difficult to conduct these one-man shows.

While dribblers should be taught to keep their vision focused outward rather than downward, they cannot be as free to look around and behind them as the boy who does not have the ball. The ball should be kept moving from one player to another, to prevent double teaming. Double teaming occurs usually when a ball handler is guarded by one man, and another one slips up undetected behind him. If the ball is kept moving, this danger is minimized. Undue speed in getting the ball from man to man is not necessary. Cool, steady, calculated speed is the type that is best used.

5. Take only sure shots

Many a freeze has been ruined because a player "thought" he could score even though he was a little off balance and fifty feet from the goal. Such a player is an impulse player and should not be given an opportunity to gamble with the team's success again. Of course, there is no such thing as a sure shot, but, certainly, there are shots that will result in an extremely high percentage of scores. These are the shots to take. An area should be designated from which shots are permissible. This area may be called the key hole, the head of the circle inward area or, as we sometimes call it, the "wash tub" area. That means that the shooter must be within the range thus specified, on balance, unhurried and taking a shot that he normally uses.

6. Use your best ball handlers

By the nature of basketball, certain men become better ball handlers than others. Guards usually bring the ball into play and have a better chance to develop ball handling skills to a high degree. Centers and forwards may develop such skills, but their chances are not as good as the guards' chances. All five men will need to be brought into the freeze system to prevent double teaming. An opponent who feels secure in the knowledge that his man is not a threat will create a lot of trouble. Each man must be a threat, but each man does not have to handle the ball an equal amount of time. There are several systems whereby two or three men do most of the ball handling.

We are going to offer *one* freeze method. It is not the only one. This system exploits all the basic principles of a good freeze. It should be taught just as any other team offense is taught. Parts and breakdown drills should be conducted before the whole thing is put together. It should be observed in its entirety, with a possible walk through before the breakdown drills are conducted, so that the players will have an idea what they are practicing. We will call this system the Tandem Post Freeze.

The Tandem Post is thus labeled because two post men are lined up in tandem position. Players #4 and #5 represent the two post men. Actually, these men can be guards or forwards but usually they are two taller players. #3 represents the team's best ball handler. He will always play one wing spot or the other and is the only one to receive the ball at a wing spot. He should be a very good faker, passer and driver. #1 and #2 will always play the point and/or the wing opposite #3. They are completely interchangeable at those two spots, rotating from point to wing to point. #1 passes to #3, the constant ball handler at a wing spot. #1 then breaks, using a reverse cut, off the hip of #4. If #1 cannot take a return pass for a lay-up under the goal, he will drift on to the corner, taking his man out of the thick of the action. Notice the strenuous fake and break by #3 in receiving. #4 is playing wide enough so that if #3's fake is not taken by his defensive man, #3 can go on in for a pass or a lay-up. The fake must be taken, resulting in his being able to receive rather easily from the point man. #4 and #5 always line up off center from the constant wing man, #3.

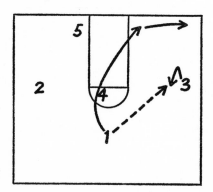

ILLUSTRATION 154.

If #3 cannot pass to #1 under the goal, he will pass back out to the point position. #3 does not dribble but will fake with head, shoulders and one foot to keep his defensive man back far enough for passing purposes. If his defensive man does not take the fake, #3 may drive in for a lay-up.

To be open for the pass at the point position, #2 fakes strongly toward the goal and cuts off a screen set by the high post man, #4. #4 rolls to the basket after #2 passes, to prevent his defensive man from interfering with the pass to #2. #4 may be wide open for a lay-up pass right under the basket. As soon as #4 passes him, #5 breaks up to take #4's free throw line spot, except that he goes to the opposite side. If #4 does not get a pass under the goal, he remains just outside the lane and plays the deep post position for the same series to be run to the other side of the floor.

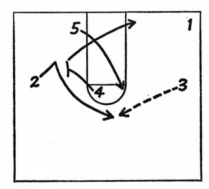

ILLUSTRATION 155.

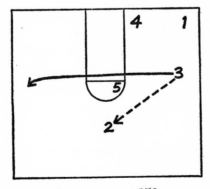

ILLUSTRATION 156.

After #3 passes back to the new point man, he breaks across the floor, cutting close to the high post man. He takes the same wing position on the other side of the floor. #1 moves up to the wing spot #3 has vacated.

#2 will pass to #3, break off the screen set by the high post man, and the entire series will be run to the left side.

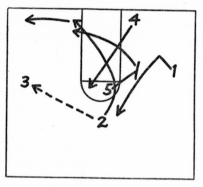

ILLUSTRATION 157.

If a team has three ball handlers of equal ability, they might vary this procedure slightly. To run the variation, #2 could return pass to the same wing spot he receives from, except that the spot would be occupied by #1. The series would then be run again to the same side of the floor. It would continue over and over to that side. The receiver would always be in a corner and have plenty of room to fake and move up for a pass.

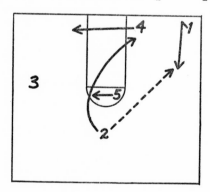

ILLUSTRATION 158.

There are many other ball control series that you may choose from. We have offered this method as an example. The important consideration is that your team should be prepared to maintain sure possession of the ball if it becomes mandatory. Careful preparation must be made for all conceivable game time emergencies. A system of ball control would surely rank high on a list of such preparations.

TEACHING HINTS

1. Keep the ball moving and do not allow excessive dribbling.
2. Stay away from danger areas.
3. Avoid cross-court and long passes.
4. Take only high percentage shots.
5. Don't start the freeze too soon.
6. Use your best ball handlers as much as possible.
7. Avoid crossing maneuvers where the ball is involved.
8. Always break to meet passes.
9. Use a method that offers the threat of scoring at any time.
10. Develop a method that is flexible, that can be varied if the situation demands adjustment.

Conclusion

Nearly all experienced coaches will be well informed, technically, concerning every subject presented in this book. For such men, it is hoped that the material presented here will serve as a reminder. For others, this basic manual should serve as a stimulus to unleash their individual contributions to the game of basketball.

If you are a good coach, you are a good teacher. Good coaching is good teaching. If you cannot teach, forget about the big trophies. They will never reside in your trophy case. Each coach should be familiar with the laws of learning and should have a thorough understanding of the word "Motivation." I refer you to the chapter entitled "Planning Your Daily Practice" in *Encyclopedia of Basketball Drills* for hints on the fundamental side of basketball teaching. These, combined with your knowledge of the learning process, should help you to produce efficient, economical practice sessions.

Fundamentals are the tools of basketball; without them no offensive system will work successfully. For the practice of each fundamental there is a right way. The coach should not allow inefficient techniques to be performed, just because they are more comfortable to the performer. He must have the courage to teach in a positive way.

Repetition of *correct* techniques is the only way to develop the fundamental tools. There is no easy way. Good teaching, close supervision and constant correction for endless hours will bring the development of good playing habits. Practices filled with horseplay, practices dedicated to having fun, practices designed to lend variety to the sessions will result in a funny, varied, clowning team. They will not result in a championship team.

The team that spends all its time on offensive practice has not begun to tap its potential strength. It has developed only half its abilities. *Defense* is the only stable element of the game. Good defense will carry you through that night when everything else fails. Strong defense will pull a group of boys together and create good morale and team courage for the close ones.

No offensive system is good without correct execution of the fundamentals. Nor will any offensive system work if fundamentals are not properly presented over a long period of time, by a progressive and gradual procedure. The *part* method of teaching a system will bring the best results. Breakdown drills should be repeated endlessly until the habits are so strong that the players will run their routes automatically, if the team is a pattern team. Free lance teams will want to work just as hard on the basic moves they want their players to make.

Be sure that your team is prepared for every eventuality. The practice schedule should embrace every phase of the game. Freezing methods, jump ball situations and other tactical situations should be prepared for as assiduously as sound defensive play.

Lastly, never forget that each player is an individual. He has talents, qualities, thoughts that are uniquely his own. He may be an X or an O in your system, but he wants and must receive treatment as an individual in the actual practice environment.

Index